pre|dispositions:
affirmations on loving

Tim'm T. West

Published in the United States in 2015 by

Red Dirt Publishing

Copyright © 2015 by Tim'm T. West

All rights reserved. No part of this publication may be reproduced, stored in a retrieval system, or transmitted by any means (electronic, mechanical, photocopying, recording, or otherwise), without the prior permission in writing of the author or publisher, or be otherwise circulated in any form of binding or cover other than that which it is published and without a similar condition including this condition being imposed on the subsequent publisher.

For information about permission to reproduce selections from this book, email:

Permissions:
Tim'm T. West
Red Dirt Publishing
tim.apostrophe.m@gmail.com
www.reddirt.biz

ISBN: 978-0-9748143-5-3

Book cover art by ArtoniWorld.com
Front and back cover photography by Rich Williams Photography
pre|dispositions is co-edited by Christina Accomando, Pam Iverson, Tonya Netjes, Nancy Olson, and William Sermons

Introduction by: L. Michael Gipson

Contents

Dedication	x
Author's Preface	xii
Introduction by L. Michael Gipson	xiii

his|story

front porches	1
wet	2
lost and found	4
why I love black men	6
pre|dispositions	8
Waking (or the haunting familiarity of a past present)	11
triggers	13
without him	14
Bisexual Blues: A confession to an ex-girlfriend, myself, or God	16
archealogy	20
differend	23

father|hood

keepsake	29
shaybutta haiku	32
mineZ	33
apparent	37
Mother's Day 2013	39
The Objectification of Freedom: A Dad's Feminist Awakening	42

book|marks

A Saving Grace	47
Open Letter to Frank Ocean	50
Reflections on Teaching (notes from a Papa Bear)	52
Expectations: A note after a "trying" day in classes	56
Why It's Personal: mPowerment and Public Health Leadership	57
Post e-race . . . izm	61
Why I'm with Teach For America	65
Inspiration as intervention: Cornelius' interview with Tim'm	68

in|between

in between	75
closer in the distance	78
weak moments	81
space	82
hibernation	84
morning epiphany in Houston	87
latex	89
causality	90
medicine	91
beautiful aftermath	92
almost	95

desire|ability

blanket	101
repetition (or daydreams about my wedding day)	104
courage!!!	106
tongue-tied	108
wait-less	110
Vow	112
him'm	113
On being-in-love (a humanifesto for the single)	114
revolution, love . . .	118
sense-ability (or the inevitability of falling)	120
admission	122
fall of mankind	124
evidence II	127
laws of physics	129
fault-lines	133

every|thing

God loves me too! (a meditation on Christianity)	139
liturgy	143
saints bracelet	145
bruise	148
even on Sundays	150
Sunday hymn for him	152
Meditations on Jesus Songs	154
half-full	160
Kuumba	161

he|art

emergency contact	165
gumbo	167
A Meditation on Happiness	169
imprint	172
golden	173
skin	175
lessons in falling: #8	177
chicken noodle	178
apology	180
how to make war after peace	182
why	184
best hug ever	186

About the author   187

pre|dispositions
affirmations on loving

Dedication

beautiful soul with feet that dance like dandelions
a laugh with pitch that echoes the songs on front porches
who painted the black and big-eyed most beautiful
for the ways they surely reflected the magic of you . . .
why so soon?
what do we do with this loss and ache, beyond remember?
and perhaps that is the point; and you live through each song,
each dance, each time we dare to color the world
through the prism of your eyes.
we recycle as gratitude.

Jermaine "Maine" Dion Smith
August 14, 1973 – March 14, 2015

Author's Preface

I am creatively spiritual, ancestrally-inspired, intellectually insatiable, a wordsmith, country-cosmopolitan, boondock-brohemian, Irma Pearl's boy, Renaissance man, hip hop head and scholar, imperfectly perfect, my own superhero, black-maled feminist, lover and fighter, dad to one and daddy to many, point-guard, papa-bear, youth advocate, maverick, Coach West, Arkansas-raised, the breath of red-dirt clay, preacher's kid, stereotype nightmare, full-moon lullaby, activist, always in love, poetically indefinable, always becoming . . .

Today I had the honor of taking a moment out to organize my fifth book, *pre|dispositions*. Going through old work was an emotional few hours: being reminded of the his|story, father|hood, book|marks, in|between, desire|ability, every|thing, and he|art that has defined my life since my last collection of unpublished work in 2007. Reading stuff so deeply personal for me is like reading the courageous moments of someone else, so a few things shocked me, and a few things I'd conveniently forgotten, not the least of which was the extent to which love and loving has so defined my journey, whether for men, or women, or my daughter, or teaching, or whatever I understand as God.

On the eve of Valentine's Day, I received a call from a love informing me that he wasn't the man to keep me happy and was leaving. A few weeks after, I received news of Maine's death (my best friend during college): unexpected, mysterious, and as haunting as hurtful. Through editing this book, I was reminded that I have been in this place before: the heartbreak, the loss. It offers affirmation that each time, I'll get through it. It is a timely "release" even for me.

A few times, not being much of a crier, I cried for him: someone not myself who survived it all. Then I honored myself enough to cry for me. It marked the unification of two selves who have historically sometimes been at war with each other; and who have finally resolved to make peace with it all. What else does self-forgiveness look like? How do we marvel, wrestle with, and affirm those things that mark attributes we gain by nature or nurture? So yes, once brave enough to put these pieces together, I cried as tribute to someone not just resilient enough to live through it, but brave enough to share. I'm better now for that. You might be too. Prepare yourself for quite a ride.

March 2015 | Washington, DC

Introduction
By L. Michael Gipson

I don't like poetry. Or rather, I don't like much of what passes as poetry. You know the kind: inaccessibility passing as depth, the esoteric and obscure masquerading as a higher aesthetic, and the florid scenting mounds of bull—"shut yo' mouf." The handful of poets I bother to read and enjoy don't try to mask through unyielding language: Gwendolyn Brooks, Langston Hughes, Essex Hemphill, Assoto Saint, Audre Lorde, Paul Beatty, Tim'm West . . . No, the poets I like to read reveal through language, exposing soft underbellies with words that open up the piece to me and vibrate within my spirit in harmony to my soul. The words call and respond to memories of experiences past and present powerfully, viscerally. These are poets I can fuck with.

Being a social media junkie, I also want a poet whose lines are so clear, true, and immediate that they can be tweeted and made a Facebook post, and instantly me and my tribe can all sigh and swoon together over the swings and connects of the poet's testifying. We hear you and we agree, and in our agreement we are made to love you. These are the poets I can fuck with.

A Renaissance man with passion A.D.H.D., Tim'm T. West also just happens to be more than a poet. He's also more than just an accomplished scholar, essayist, a lyrical prose writer, an activist, a father, a seeker, a bisexual, a bear chaser, a man—he's a curious creative being with a message calling. How this Mercury delivers his message depends on the mood of those on high whispering to this vessel. Some scoff at the thought of an artist being good at delivering these calling cards of the Gods through more than one means, but I prefer my mediums with a ravenous appetite for multiple forms, studies, subjects, platforms, and protest movements, exhibiting Durga-like hands extending to touch, reach, lift multiple people from the mundane and the miserable through art born of insatiability and concern. And throughout *pre|dispositions* we see a portrait of a mid-life artist concerned with so very many heady subjects, so many messages to transport. Through exposure to tireless self-examination, we are made privy to his furrowed brows about manhood, about fatherhood, about faith, God, and service, about being a survivor standing (though sometimes kneeling) amidst a sea of premature graves.

In his public displays of self-affection (and sometimes self-flagellation), West teaches us how to be concerned without shame, interrogate without blinking, reflect with grace and forgiveness, place unsure footing forward despite fears, and most of all to love with courage, with self-love being the most courageous and yet most difficult of political and personal acts. West makes no bones about the Kilimanjaro climb of that most sacred and necessary act, and of the broken knees and scarred hands suffered from the progress made up and the cyclical, inevitable slides down. We need that unflinching honesty about those busted knees and bloodied hands at a time when self-help is too often described as a destination arrived to by sheer force of will, prayer, tarrying and/or fasting, and once arrived: "voilà," permanent lifetime residency. Ha! If only it were so. West illustrates how loving one's self is not a nirvana achieved, but an unruly garden in need of constant tending and affection.

This book presents much about the tools, experiences, and observations West has accumulated in his self-work. Over forty years inhaling and exhaling this poisonous American air that would choke his Black, gay body dead, he illustrates how to dare to be, think, and question out loud. In sharing his struggle to find internal and external filters for clean air to clear his mind and spirit, to have oxygen required for the heavy lifting of asphyxiated others, he provides breadcrumbs to paths one should and shouldn't take for their own breath beat.

In his fervent concern for him and us at times, like most Black evangelists in testimony, he tells us too much, but better that, to talk us into living, than the crippling silence of stoic performance that has become all the masculine rage in our ritual suicide of "I'm fine. I'm good. Everything is everything with me" until it's not, until we're not. Falling like human dominoes of denial into the abyss, we need the bridges and scaffolding of broad shoulders, healing hands, and over-sharing mouths to remind us how to crossover to truth, to stand, be, do, and think out loud again unapologetically, with bracing honesty. Everything is not all right. We are not okay, fine, good . . . No. Too many are sliding, no rushing into that sweet dark night to say otherwise, too anxious to leave this plane, to meet God up close with angry questions. We need reminders, or as West says, triggers of the beauty and purpose of this space and why our place in it matters. Why the unique God within each of us here is a light undeserving of early extinction. "Keep it lit," says West, one breath at a time. West is a messenger I can fuck with.

L. Michael Gipson, BFA, MS, is an award-winning writer, public health, and youth advocate, who has worked on HIV/AIDS, youth and community development programming for 21 years. The Music Editor at SoulTracks.com, an Associate Editor at Lambda Literary, and a Red Dirt Press author, Michael's articles, short stories, and essays have been multiply anthologized, most recently in "For Colored Boys Who've Considered Suicide When The Rainbow Is Not Enough (Magnus Books)." A Chicago native, he works and resides in Detroit. MI.

his|story

"Isn't the ability to edit our lives
among the more beautiful things about living?" —TTW

front porches

rusty, crooked
ashy elbows and
chapped lips
carry legacy;
sop stories up
'bout belonging and not . . .

I've inherited
the lips of secrets
not told to me
whisperin' to me
in winds
between woods
and houses they build:

"remember where you came from
. . . remember the red in your melanin
like your feet remember
the texture
of this here red clay"

so I do . . .
writing
is remembering.

wet

I'd like to become
more wet
again

boys are raised
to be concrete
poured soft
they harden
where earth
would have softened them.

but time
being faster than boys' feet can race
chases them into being men.

erect like monuments
these towers of babel
these tragic phallic fallacies
confuse the language of love
with the language of power.

so sun, wind, rain
and the elements
like tears that don't get released
almost always
leave these buildings–
formed of stubborn impatience
and domination–
broken.

all hardened things
eventually
break.

I want to raise a peace flag
place it on my pole
surrender this hardness
that has killed me
to protect me.
become soft again
like in the womb:
wet.

lost and found

there are parts of me I lose
packing boxes:
my life
best knowable
through books I've collected and keep . . .
photographs, theory, poetry
thread my fragility
hold my "making sense"
together
are the library of me
psychoanalytic canon
a biography of thought and desire
edited with scrutinizing urgency.
self-loving . . .
especially because I forget to be.

damn right . . .
I produce a history of me
worth reading.

there are parts of me I gain
leaving things behind
for a moment or years
gaps I have to feel with memory
damaged recollection
or disremembrance
the echo's faint disapperance
stronger in the distance
the archeologist's discovery
of something looked for
found first in the heart's mind . . .
so I lose myself in the stacks
to find myself . . . better.

there are parts
rediscovered
I'd rather keep boxed.
found again
they haunt
until I forgive my own betrayal
books are heavy
can weigh you down.

and yes,
a few times in life
I've given up on me
stop reading and writing
ready to die.
so for those who, like me,
need to read and write
as sure as next breaths come
I wonder:
if our books bear testimony
to lives we've led and will lead
who are we becoming?
what should we read next?
why read,
if not to map a curriculum
to joy?

is anything
lost in the heart
anything but the soul's library
longing to breathe again
born again
in the excavation
of stories.

why I love black men

because I believe in blood memory
see him best
in the dark
the cacophony of chains
a lullaby
sense the desperation of being lost
at sea
floating
stacked next to
on top of
beside him
felt him dying
tasted him crying
prayed he would live to see me
in light again

because there was a time
the only way I knew I was living
was his breath on my flesh
this salt, this depth, this passion
a testimony
that we would only survive
if strong
a test of resilience
different ships, same boat
time bending forward
beyond middle passages
still gripping his hand
for dear life
until his skin began
to feel like mine

because he has seen me
hung
Mandingo
strange fruit
gun shots, hunting dogs
faggots.

because salt is a texture
with grit like Africa
and I am black
and sometimes blue
and choose to love a black man
because I can
remember.

pre|dispositions

I bite
my bottom lip
anxious or angry,
eat late night
in boxers
whatever I please:
strange plate-fellows.
feel proud when I belch
or fart . . .
loud   alone
glare back
at niggas that glare
talk shit on basketball courts
knowing
braggadocio
on a good day
can make lucky shots
look intentional.

these days
I do too much
alone
on purpose
avoiding predispositions.
work and play
sometimes
alone
on purpose
grateful
I didn't become a man
with more answers
than questions

rules I create
to rule others
while not ruling myself
pleased
I ain't got ten kids
to fan away bad gas
clearin' the room
with Bible and baritone
and with some woman
cookin' for me
'cause she fell in love
I didn't deserve
and afraid
to blow my cover
keepin' her
hinged to hope
feeding
the hunger:
my fragile ego's
insatiability.

there where I cry
for another to feel
where I try not to smile
but fail
I got predispositions
I dig:
young men and grown boys
looking for father-figures
gravitate to my tone
girl-chil'ren
wishin' they were stars
but afraid of night
call me papa bear
unprompted
sense the growl in the gut

know I'll blow a house down
sting like a bee
eat my spinich
leap tall bigots
in a single frown
and pity the fool
who would blow my cool
to protect mineZ.

have worked
my whole life
to keep the best parts
at heart
celebrate the cuts I've made
to bleed true
honor
whatever I'm honing
and keep
that other shit
to myself
deal with the unwanted
unshakable
predispositions
'til they get disremembered
like dreams
you forget
cuz it hurts to be reminded
they get lost.

and I wake
happy I have become
the better man I'm becoming . . .

alone
on purpose.

Waking
(or the haunting familiarity of a past present)

Waking up is a Lalah Hathaway ballad serenading a dream through a jammed alarm clock. It mocks her contralto even as it does not disturb its perfection. It's looking carefully for just the right moment to get beyond opened eyelids to fuller presence: shower-rain, toothbrush, the ouch of warm feet on cold morning tile. Waking seems crudely impossible, if necessary, in the way that some people find the courage to die or like taking medicine that makes you sick to keep you from getting sick.

He watched the intervals pass: six-fifty-one, six-fifty-five—all the while knowing that his life was fifteen minutes faster than it was supposed to be. He was one of those cats who wanted to outrun the future so he'd feel safer. He wanted to master the science of time and interaction, so that nothing would catch him off guard. He wanted the calculus of life simplified as a basic fraction—not half-empty or half-full, just half. Just half wouldn't feel happy or sad. He would be spared the bite of extremities. Neither heaven nor hell seemed places he'd want to retire his spirit, so he waited a few minutes more before spinning his body around to meet crisp air awaiting him bare, outside of comforters.

His room was predictable, orderly in a way that masked dust lingering about the space. It was an ambitious if private IKEA showroom. He diligently choreographed the space, as repetitious and stubborn to change as his ears were for Incognito's "Deep Water." There was a disturbing addition to the kind of blues that created more shadow than light in this room without windows. But there was sunlight: his poetry, the shine off his computer, pictures of people who loved him dancing about the walls.

Most of the rooms he'd slept in all his life had that same feel—except for the room he shared with his ex. There were lots of things he missed about that room; about having to suspend the certainty of how it'd be found, like the imprint of his lover's nap there upon coming home. Loving somehow helped him get over this delusion of predictability. But that was his old life—it had escaped his consciousness on purpose. He simply disremembered it. Those memories haunted him, reminded him of the ways his heart had tricked or failed him. The guise of cool and resolve has a habit of snapping him awake—waking him up at three-thirty a.m., reminded that he hates sleeping alone—hates the hollow echo of clock ticking or the couple upstairs stirring into and out of boot-knocking.

He once met a therapist with a crazy theory that super-orderly people create order in spaces to offset the chaos they experience with things they can't control: who they love, those loud glances at Metro stops, people with intentions to mask evil in blue suits. It simply wasn't that deep for him. This room, this safe-sanctuary was one of the few things that had never failed him, left him lonely, overburdened with his affections.

triggers

triggers
need a finger
a word or memory
that hurt you.
and the only
real option
to escape the pain
is the prospect of a peace
that threatens to pull heavier
than your tears.

I've learned
to find hopeful triggers
in the admission
that I'm not okay
that I'm tired
that my enough doesn't seem
enough.
so then I dance enough
find song enough
football and basketball enough
I counter
or re-trigger enough
to remember
hope
is greater than my pain.
there is a smile
I deserve to see
again . . .

the stretch of my own grin
the pitch and reverb
of my own knee-slapping laughter
triggers too.

without him

(for Eric Rofes August 31, 1954 – June 26, 2006)

in his absence
we wondered what we'd do
without the words
only his mouth
knew how to say
grab, pull, and hold hands
or each other
those who share
the void
hold tighter
read between lines
to complete the story
he was writing
offer evidence
of his organic
social networking.

who would we be
today
without him?

for sometimes
one of us sounds like him
does something like him
becomes more brave
more free like him
because we remember
together

so to answer the question
often asked:
"What would Eric do?"
we realize we are doing it
in the asking
the remembering
the celebration of his life
we continue to live
remembering

what would we do without him?
exactly what his design
his cut and paste
his outlining and re-edits
dictated:
we remember
each other, while still here
remember that
in memory
there is no
"without him"
he stays, lives, breathes
in the celebration
of memory
he is the mortar
between these bricks
we continue to lay
erecting this house
always unfinished
on purpose.

Bisexual Blues:
A confession to an ex-girlfriend, myself, or God

Sweetheart,

I am writing you because I have been reading Cixous (again). She releases me from the shackles of my own fear enough to acknowledge what was and what could have become of us. We are a lost cause or short-circuited soulmates: broken before we could ever break up, so perhaps never together at all . . . and therefore always together . . . in the residue of remembrance and possibility. For what you likely see of me—reducible to Facebook updates and the "notes" I choose to share—it may seem that I have said or made more of the romantic lessons with men. In a dichotomizing society that demands that we choose, I am sometimes more of a wimp than brave—choosing to let the gravity of my resistance to interdictions and taboos shape the desirability I claim. So I have more often chosen to love men . . . at least publicly. Sad I know, huh? I do make use of the lessons you taught. Long time coming.

When I am most free, I have chosen not to choose men over women (or vice versa), understanding the agile and dynamic nature of choice: the choice, like YOU and ME, could have been something Other. But we are not. There is no we to speak of except when I go to the Post Office and your Uncle senses the sadness waiting to come undone behind the guise of pleasantries. He always calls me out; stumbles over my stuttered name. And I somehow remember your lips at those moments. I sometimes regret going to get mail. He knows both a little and a lot about us. A little from what I told him. A lot for all the telling my silence surrenders. Sometimes I think you are not so much one that got away, or even a regret, as you are a presence that lingers. To be sure, I don't believe for a moment in a day that we were any match made in heaven. Such idealism has always failed me. I seek the match made right here on earth—perfect imperfections bravely in full-view—especially for me and whomever becomes my better whole. I do believe that you and I left indelible impressions on each other, even in the one moment worth forgetting.

Truth is, there are times when I miss you. And I hate it, like I hated being afraid to love you in a world that would have mistaken my choice for cure. I chose my virulent disdain for the heteronormativity that chokes boys like me over YOU. I chose to refuse the possibility of becoming a man who hurts women, so I hurt you trying not to. I made of my desire to cuddle and be nearer and next to you an ontological proof. Where emotions get out of control, I turn to reason. No reason for it except fear. In the hierarchy of the work I have been called to do, I chose affect over your effect, pushed you away when you wanted to be closest to me. Disremembered who you were for the social implication and burden of being in love with a woman: the insidiously bigoted heterosexual praise, the gay shame. In the final equation, I did not desire the luxury of partnership with a woman in a world that would have pathologized me as DL, hiding, confused, a freak, or sexually greedy.

And so I have become a man who gets hurt by men. And it's not that I don't love or am not capable of loving men. It's just that there are things about the men I love that I believe restricts the possibility of the kind of union you seem to enjoy now with your husband. When big dogs bark at big dogs, their bark distracts from the harmony that could exist between them, becomes a monotone mantra of braggadocio and ego. I try. I am learning. Maybe I need a puppy, or need to be a puppy. But there are sensibilities I've felt with women that are unique and special. I have recognized them in some men, though they are all too afraid to admit it, preferring bravado and stoicism over being the big softies that catch my attention in the first place. Game recognizes game. I know this because it's the reason any of them have fallen for me. A man not terribly invested in manhood, if enjoying sports, ciphers, and playin' papa bear, I am one who longs to cry far more than I do, whose favorite verb is cuddle, and whose only distraction from ESPN is Haagen Dazs or the spot on a lover's neck meant for my lips.

Today I am as afraid of loving as I was back when I struggled to love you but didn't quite know how to. My body was sweating and malfunctioning for having submitted to a previous (male) lover who, not being honest with himself, left my body with a reminder. I can't say I absolutely knew it then—knew what it was in my body that was struggling against the ways you wanted me inside of you—but I am today glad I chose to break something replaceable—thrown against a wall in my frustration about the impending failure—than to have broken your heart or complicated your life. I was wrong for throwing my phone across the room (if not in your direction), but another of your kisses may have made me a criminal or monster. Women before YOU and since have been safe with me. I regret that moment. I should have handled it differently . . . found the words . . . created the words. Gone for the plunge? This world didn't have the words to describe that which cannot be defined. I failed for trying.

It wasn't all me. I'm not sure you ever saw me as a man. As feminist and free as the pillow where theory meets the bedroom, you seemed to desire a man who'd be "man" with you . . . and for all my physical prowess and baritone, I tend to be most manly with men. Women I desire turn me into a lesbian. It is there where I've been most at ease with the personal politics of submission. My kiss was too soft for you. And for all the ways my tongue may have tickled you . . . I was seldom truly interested in hitting that, banging you, or knocking boots; even less interested in bragging to my "boys" about it. I refuse rather than confuse the language of violence with that of a love's softness. All but a few black women expect their men to be 100 percent heterosexual, if free-spirited. I am not sure you are any different, even in your proverbial and theoretical queerness. Queerness made you sexy. It made me a faggot. And I see the ways photographs now paint you as picture perfect and happy—a portrait I surely would have refused for all the color it hides. You have what the sistahs call a "real man"— something I have never aspired to be. Realness trips over itself. I'm as real as they get for not giving a damn about keeping up appearances. Maskulinity takes far too much work; so many needless iterations of bravado for a brotha who prefers the warmth and familiarity of womb-magic. Perhaps this is why I have always needed women close to me—especially those not terribly invested in their Femininity. I'm not your typical "real" man. Cute in theory, huh? Not so cute with flesh, bone, and a pulse. (smile)

If you have made me out to be a monster, it is because you remember how safe it felt to be held by me, remember my heartbeat, lose your breath in our breathing together, and that you know nothing could be further from the truth . . . and need to resist the memory. You know me. The space between us confirms it. The last time I saw you confirmed it—your husband's abjectifying mean-mug and your withdrawal confirmed it. True to form, I desired you then and there too. I suppose he too would have been cute if he were not frowning. Part of me wanted to buck up to him, the other part of me wanted to shake his hand or offer a hug. I did neither. I left you both . . . alone.

My freedom to love men enabled my freedom to love women of my choosing. Not some compulsory desire driven by fear of the complications, misunderstandings, or intolerance of friends, family or society. So it is important that people know that I loved you and other women like you—if clearly no better at it than my careless attempts to find peace with men. I once had fantasies of black bohemian love grounded by picnic blankets, organic fruit, a baby, and a Negritude anthology or one of Octavia Butler's *Parables*. And perhaps someday I'll meet a sista or brotha (of whatever color) who "gets" me enough to forget me. And this will free me to be who I am supposed to be—if grossly loyal and loving in the most cliché ways. Yes there will be poetry, and music, and dance and color . . . but I no longer hold my breath for that. I'm just certain of what love isn't. It isn't being with a woman who considers me a failure because some men make me blush. It also isn't a guy who thinks holding onto me is the surest way to ensure I don't change. I am today grappling with the very hard questions about what romantic love in my life could look like; I dare say nonconventional, though there are surely ways I will be conventional. Preoccupation with avoiding convention is all too conventional. I want a wedding, a big cake, my family and friends present, and a spot in JET magazine. Among the greatest gifts I have are my dreams. Call me a rebel.

Woman with the pretty smile. Loving you was among the times I felt most free—shameless about the expanse of my desirability—even when it meant disciplining it in order to embrace a YOU free enough to love a free ME. I'm growing stronger in my resolve that desirability is only as vast as the imagination allows. No longer bound by any ontological determinability of Eros that defies the very dynamic and fluid nature of romantic desire regardless of which prefix one chooses to use to label my sexuality, I become freer to wander where the blood beats strongest, if anywhere. So today I sit with me. Today I explore the patience needed to rediscover the courage of a fearless spirit . . . in love.

For all I don't know, I am certain of a few things, despite the disbelief of people on both sides who feel compelled to confine me to some determinable hermeneutics of my poetry. Contrary to popular belief, I quite often mince words, so nosy or speculating interpreters and translators always fail. Those who know me, don't try to . . . they realize that they can't. That's the fun part. I love the real friends. They understand that the actuality of my desire for men and women is one of the few certainties for which I can vouch. It's like God. I believe, but don't ask for any specifics beyond the ways it materializes in my gut, spirit, or libidinal impulses. And though we do not speak beyond the awkward moments when I slip and check out your Facebook page . . . or when I try to say something nice to be assured no response, I thank you for enabling me to be the realest man I have become. Something reminded me of us today: a trip hop song, the color of the sky, a pretty woman's smile, a trip to the post office. Damn you!

archaeology
(for Antione)

what do you do
when someone digs you
so intently
breaks stone
gets fingernails dirty
blows away earth and ash
with reassuring whisper
to find you
fixed
between the coal
of your wait
hiding from your best self
afraid of being discovered
as priceless?

what do you give
a friend
who each day
gives his all
to know you're good . . .
gives everything
then goes and gets some more
so you remember
you are worth
more than your memories
more than your pain or fears
the ways they bind
and block
your blessings?
How do you wrap the gift
that is your heart
exposed?

this is what you do . . .
you remember:
your greatest loves
have sometimes
never been lovers . . . and that's okay.

you try
each day
to be a man who makes him proud
hustle hard
face your fears
make love through art
open the lock to pandora's box
bravely
expose, to the world
the courage that makes you
vulnerable.
you dig yourself enough to believe
what he already believes
you deserve:
every desire of your heart
can be yours.
so you believe in his
belief in you
having faith in him
a best friend
without condition.

and you praise God
when he smiles.
and you push him
hardened
to be softer.
you pray for him
when he doubts
the efficacy of prayer.
you keep him close
even when he gets
under your skin.
tell him everything;
never being afraid
of being bare, if broken.

sometimes
a diamond
a bone
a keepsake
polished

shines better
as evidence
of a life
that got lost
to someday be found
as priceless.

differend
(for lenny yorke: August 31, 1962 - November 15, 2008)

"there is no non-phrase
silence is a phrase
there is no last phrase"

— jean francois lyotard
_____

today, I am not a poet
for missin' words
to describe the ways I miss him
so here is the poem

each time another passes
a gaping hole is left
I have outlived too many
of my own angels
thick and brown with care
like molasses
if unable to hold wings together.
the memories stick
and I am among the sweet who remain
delighting in the beautiful way
memories haunt
when angels fly back into sky
and flesh becomes dust.

conversations and secrets
whispered to myself
he held
now . . . gone
Orion cries
stars blink clearer tonight
are the remains of whatever we were
illuminate the absence of language
to describe
this absence.

the flood-rush of all this pain
I fear feeling.
feeling is not my friend
the friends who truly "get me"
who make no apology for synchronicity
of smile or flirtation
keep leavin' me . . . alone.

safety being too rare a luxury
in the world
I need to re-shield
for my own protection
for the loss of my soul brotha
who held a mirror to parts of me
in his eyes
so I fear
I will never look
as beautifully shameless
bare and broken
all of me delicately held together
with bruise and sweat
again.

and each time I receive news
that a part of me has died
I am left a little less
and a little more
human.
less for the ways I refuse to recover
more for all the ways I'll try anyhow
tongue too numb to sing my own lullaby
hands failing to write
neuropathy beyond fingertips
blockage of tear ducts
eyes repress
the undescribably hollow reality
of the savior I can no longer call
except to pray
and know
he is evidence of God
when family and friends
rebuke me.

today
unsure 'bout what to feel
except to know what it means
to lose someone
irreplaceable
again
I may break
become the brave soul
he knew and loved
but today I am frail and afraid
I am not quite me
for missin' him.
and perhaps
all the more myself
without words
if able to conjure hope
try if failing to cry.

today, I am not a poet
for missin' words
to describe the ways I miss him
so here is the poem.

father|hood

"Spank the hands of a child taking baby steps, and she'll never learn to walk. Encourage her crawling . . . head lifted sometimes towards an unknown destination, the pitter patter of hands and feet pushing her wait into futurity—her somewhere-over-the-rainbow—and she'll remember it when she begins to walk, run, fly!" —TTW

keepsake
(for Shay)

I do not have much
but leave you this . . .

1.
do better than this
lifestyle of the broke(n) and "brilliant"
a healer
understand your gift
is rare
they will magnify
your magnificent magnetism
pulled, puller, pillar
they will be drawn to you
draw you
without fault-lines
though you, perfectly imperfect,
quake and quiver sometime
you know better:
the gravity of wars
waged through your heart
can crack and crumble pillars
so you too.

honor this enough
to be human:
the break-downs, the tears
the moments alone that feel
like years
and lessons in falling
are what most beautifully
shape
you.

2.
restore yourself shamelessly
exhalt and offer praise
for the ways you find strength
to stand . . .withstand
stand with . . . ALL.

for you are all there is
and nothing at all, but God, exists
without you.
still
in your safe-guarding
independence:
remember you need Others
as they surely need you.

dance often
rhythm will remind you
that you are weightless.
when stuck?
float!

3.
be prepared to die
each day
knowing you have lived
beautifully
for what is more beautiful
than courage?

I learned at 12
2/4/85
years before you were born
Grandma Ellen
smiled to me from her bed
said she loved me
said Goodbye.

she never said Goodbye.

I smiled back . . .
through a single tear.
her life
not without worry or burden
a perfect life still
a dream fulfilled
so she had made her peace.
make your peace
each day.

and never wonder
about the wonder
you are becoming
ancestors are unseen angels
shadow you in dark places
on dark days
direct the path to light.
never for a moment forget
you are love
love is you
love is all there is . . .

for I am just the man
you call dad
and I do not have much
but leave you this . . .
words on a page
written with hands
a bit stronger than
my heart
today:

a prayer
a piece of me
a keepsake.

shaybutta haiku

sometimes, yeah sometimes
thinkin' I got nobody
she texts: "love you, dad"

mineZ

lately
I'm being asked a lot
if she's my biological
as if biology follows
the logic of care
as if it is
a parent.

nosy like noses of bloodhounds
on a trail of underground kinship
they complicate the contrast
in our complexions
look for something
in the eyes
the smile
the bloodline
that might authenticate
that she's actually mineZ.

and it frustrates me
to no end
that I have to qualify
my next of kin
by anything other than saying:
"she's my daughter."

I have suggested
that while blood
may be thicker than water
blood without water
dries
is no less than a biological
diabolical lie
and this logic
that any man who can spit seed
or any woman who can breed
is necessarily parent material
ain't so apparent
to me.

so they examine the names:
Matesky ain't West
but both contain EST
suffix meaning ultimate,
like our bond:
bestest
greatest
like you ask the stupidest questions.
Flip the M in Matesky
and you got double-u
so all you need to know is that both
Matesky and West be,
blessed, G.

'cause you are doing way too much work
to try to make non-sense
of common sense:

She needed her dad.
I showed up.
unlike some blood relatives
more concerned with getting
tore up
than the know whats:
is she safe?
does she need some money?
are her teachers good?
when was the last time she smiled . . .
because of me?

I be that purposeful parental figure
unlike the grateful niggas on Maury
joyous jiggaboo dancing when they hear
the opposite of their worst fear:
"you are not the father."

forget blood
I be that water. . . be waterfall,
the molecular structure of care
she knows is there when needed
so the extent to which i've seeded
is irrelevantly clear
what matters is that I'm here.

And yeah . . .
she's the only one I've got
May 2, 1988 had a heart-ache
deferred 'til my purpose became
a parent:
she, my most precious keep sake
16 year difference . . . yeah . . .
you do the math
more concerned
about which white chick i "hit"
at 15
than how i protect and nurture
my young queen
you
demeanin the meaning of kinship.

Watch her face contour
when she's happiest
the expression when somebody's testin
or she's stressin
the passion with which she spits
Uh Huh
then quit
cuz she mineZ.
notice how she glows
when loved well
and take a tip from Nas
cuz it ain't hard to tell
this spell ain't DNA
it's DNA on its backside
AND like i said:
she mineZ
case closed.

so do what you must
'til you combust
'til you configure the compulsory
will to know
yes or no
is she really . . . really?

silly.

'til your spine breaks
like my heart aches
whenever the matter matters
so much people stagger:
"you was into white girls?"
"into girls?"

all you need to know
is that I was into THAT girl
since first sighting.
There was a void
I didn't try to avoid
so I filled it
cuz I never failed it . . .
this responsibility
to assume this role
in her life
didn't require a wife
it be Moraga
familia from scratch.

so to the question
of what I must had done done
way back
Roger this
before you Roger that
there is no assurance beyond the calling
that I catch her tears falling
be a bridge
when she's crawling for drive
on this journey to find
the business
you can't seem to mind.

like any baby girl
placed in a room
with her dad
you will find
the gravity between
sightlines.

yeah:
She mineZ

apparent

dear parent,
your oblivion
to parental responsibility?
apparent.
I see your child daily
thirsty, broken, and hungry . . .
for more than the affirmation
that life began with you
on purpose . . .
and while I don't have heart enough
to fill the void
of your betrayed love
I try.

tell me . . .
what in heaven
called you to believe
putting your child out
was righteous?
what stubborn heart-lens
did you use
to translate the Bible?
the one used by King James?
does this prideful allegiance
rationalize your faithful abandon?
Is hypocritical piety
the pride you prize?

I remember from church
with pops who was pastor
even Isaac was honored
as sacrifice . . . to God
not left for dead
living.
my father who art in heaven
and my father
made, mold, and perfect
their child
love me too.

I wonder . . .
when you look in the mirror
do the lines in your face
deepen with worry
do you feel the bite of winter
on your skin
when you remember
the part of you
banished and shamed
for being
what you nurtured . . .
or chose not to?

in mirrors . . .
or in the abyss of clasped hands
do you see your child too?
feel their hunger,
hanger,
pull their trigger?
do your veins become thirsty
for hope or salvation?
when you shower
do you prepare for your body
a marketplace
bartering necessities?
how well do you sleep at night
in your bed?
does it ever feel like pavement?
or just you? petrified and hardened
by the truth:

this throwaway
is one you raised.
and being of God
is your child also not a child of God?
how do you deny blessed inheritance
when convenient?
is this not
apparent?
are you not
a parent?

Mother's Day 2013

On Mother's Day, I'll be thinking of my daughter, Shay. Our last conversation was troubled, challenging, full of so much left unsaid. We haven't talked since. Awkward. She turned 25 last week; and I suppose the challenge of how much to hold onto vs. let go, deepens. I always feel that it's a "damned if I do, damned if I don't" thing. We opted not to have the belated-birthday luncheon on 5/5—a few days deferred from the earth day 5/2. It was probably best. She invited me to stop by a party friends had that night. I got caught up in stuff at work . . . and wanted her to enjoy a gathering with friends instead. Excuse? Perhaps.

We're both workaholics, dreamers, travelers, artists, change agents. It's sometimes really hard for either of us to make time. Yet, as dad, I can't make excuses. It will almost always be my "fault" . . . and I'm having to learn to accept that. It becomes apparent to me, that for all the mentors and guides she has, I'm her parent. At 15 this meant one thing. At 25 something altogether different. I applaud and could be no more proud of all the ways she's grown since I became active in her life. There was no formula for how to engage our complicated relationship:

1. Are you happy?
2. What can I do to support that?
3. If unable, what else can I do . . . ?
4. Try to listen, let go, let grow
5. Try to always be there when called on
6. Call on her to call on. (She's fiercely and shamelessly independent, a trait which I admire)
7. Give space when needed . . . but stay close. We always reconnect best after some space.

On Mother's Day I'll think of Shay. She was not even 10 when she lost her mother. I'm sure she might recall me talking about my sole attempt at novel writing; a project with a working title "Motherless" that I've been writing . . . 10 years. It's an intense story about two children who grow up motherless. And I suppose, being one who writes poetic memoir, I found it easier to fictionalize something I could not imagine. It freed me to separate myself in ways that are challenging given that the success and praise for my writing is connected to its being acutely personal. Shannon is beginning to understand the blessing and burden of this dynamic as she travels and tours with her one-woman show: "She Think She Grown."

There's a fine line between what I feel comfortable sharing and what may embarrass her. There is no shame in our connection for me, for all the ways it's complicated. Sometimes we are too close. Sometimes I see trajectories in her becoming that make my tummy tight and make me wanna be all too protective. Sometimes I feel like a failure . . . for when I wasn't dad, for when I've tried and haven't known how to be, for continued mis-steps. Sometimes I think she wants me to be perfect instead of just love her hard, if clumsily. Sometimes I wonder if she notices that I'm trying. Lately, it has hurt a lot, not quite knowing if I've made a difference at all.

On Sunday I'll be miles away from my mother but will think of Shay. I'll wonder how she processes the day. I'll want to be there, though I cannot . . . and perhaps she's learned to be just fine with the day, and I'm just struggling with it—wanting at times to fill every void, every hurt she has ever had to experience. Sometimes I know I love her too much. Sometimes it hurts that she might ever question this, given my busy schedule and musings. I do know that whenever she's called for me to be there, I've made efforts to shuffle, make space, show up. I realize that this may not be enough. How do you compensate for years of hurt you could not be there for? The longing to be full, to have things answered, to clarify the fuzzy memories and resolve one's past is hard enough for me with clear vision and connection still to my parents. There's hope still that my healing can involve the ways my mom and dad (divorced for as long as they were together) continue to work through this journey called parenting that, I suppose, never fully stops.

On Sunday, I'll think of Shay. I'll wonder. Does she realize how much I love her, miss her. That I sometimes say nothing for failing to be the "corny dad," "too proud," "too involved," "not involved enough." We both grace magazine and newspaper covers. We both busy folk. But I do know this . . . There's no one who I trust to carry the legacy of whatever I'll leave behind, more than Shay. In that way, I need her close. And I think that's just it. I think sometimes, she fails to see that dad needs her too: uncertain, hurting, overwhelmed, struggling at times because I'm not where I thought I'd be at 40, though I've done quite a bit. I suppose I just want to know she's proud of me too. She's lived a bit. Wiser, sometimes I want to know what she thinks. And perhaps I need to accept that she might too simply wonder:

1. Are you happy?
2. What can I do to support that?
3. If unable, what else can I do . . . ?

4. Try to listen, let go, let grow
5. Try to always be there when called on
6. Call on him to call on.
7. Give space when needed . . . but stay close. We always reconnect best after some space.

On the flight to Los Angeles, I sat next to a man who was reading one of those books that some fathers are reading to create a contract with their daughter(s) to remain pure, chaste, perfected. I love my daughter through the uncertainty of her missteps, encourage her when she doesn't quite know the answers but must pretend in order to fuel her own courage. She would not have made it thus far . . . too vulnerable. She's a fighter. We're more alike than different on many levels. But sometimes I realize that we both need to make time to just sit. Be daughter and dad . . . away from those who know who she is and who I am; who we are and who we are to each other . . . and enjoy the silence. We're still both here. Different journeys, but stronger people for the ways we've showed up for each other. I'm not sure I can think of a reason worth living better than trying to be a better dad for her. She's among the strongest people I know; and I love her. I hope she knows this.

The Objectification of Freedom:
A Dad's Feminist Awakening

I have witnessed her grow into her body. Time flies. The very curves and voluptuousness that appear in my now-grown daughter were not so long ago flattened by a pre-adolescent "innocence" that was perhaps more my fantasy than my daughter's reality. It was the seemingly necessary de-sexualization of a young girl for my own "peace of mind"— a way of seeing her as sex-incapable, abstinent; girlie flirtation, at best, marked by the innocence of school girl crushes or puppy love. I would come to discover that her reality was much much different. She has grown into a woman who owns her own body—its decisions, its actions, inaction, its desirability and explorations. Is it any surprise that I helped raise a feminist, if unsure she's even comfortable with such a term and its connotations?

As I sat in the Chicago box theater's front row to see my daughter, Shannon Matesky's, developing one-woman show "She Think She Grown," any fantasy of "innocent" girlhood is shattered. While attuned to much of the hardship she encountered, particularly in the foster care system, and "pre-dad," I had no idea about some of what would be revealed to me, for the first time, on stage. This show—a therapeutic exposition of a woman brilliantly struggling to find her voice in the world, in her own grown-woman way—was masterfully executed if uncomfortable at moments to watch as someone who cares . . . who wishes I could have rescued her from some of life's hardships, or been there earlier in her life. Shay has always been independent—a quality that as a feminist-minded dad, I applaud with liberal resolve. I never cared much who Shay dated when she came of age to date, only that she was happy, not being abused, sexually responsible. I was attentive to her coming of age in high school and the necessary explorations: bisexuality, boys, her just doing her!

My principal concern was that she knew she could come to me with anything—a reassurance of my unconditional love, if with the expected paternal protectiveness. I was among the first to hear about her first college boyfriend, first major breakup, and the struggles thereafter to balance an artistic career with what becomes of desire-ability. Unlike her dad, who seems sometimes to live for loving—often to my own detriment—Shay is stridently, if stubbornly, independent; resolved that career and dreams should wait for no man or woman. I think she could stand to be a little more like me, allowing dreams of being loved well to happily coexist with creative aspirations. But then there are the realities she's witnessed of dad's trail of heartbreaks. She believes I could stand to be more like her—unwilling to allow distractions in loving to deter or shape a creative or professional future. I think we both still have a lot to learn from each other.

Our notion of family is far from traditional, but more so, as we say, like Cherríe Moraga's *familia from scratch*. Even as she is now a college graduate and adult, we continue to develop and nurture the mix we make through life's generous supply of ingredients. Single-dad, queer & grown-daughter, bisexual. We both float in the world with a magnetism that both allures and burns—like a moth to a flame. Our plays and poetry are sometimes the way we best communicate life experiences—if an oddly public call-and-response, through growth processes, both respectively and as father-daughter. It's so much more difficult to sit and talk about some of these things. We respect the stage as a mode of disclosure. Since I moved to Chicago and we talk more often we are becoming braver to have talk-backs, beyond the audience, one-on-one. So it is in this growth that I have began to struggle with certain feminist tendencies around womanhood and sexual objectification. With a daughter, I am unable to see feminism outside of the lens of my relationship to Shay, or my mother, or sisters, or nieces. And it troubles me that sexism is such an insidiously ever-present normality that I'm thought of as abnormal for trying to challenge it. I don't like that women get paid less for the same work. I hate when the value of a woman is measured through her sex or baby-making ability. I respect a woman's right to choose a destiny that I may not believe is best for her . . . because I value that same freedom. What is feminism if not about full freedom?

Being a feminist dad for me has meant not reducing my daughter's body to an object-to-be-protected . . . as some extension of my property. It's about encouraging and nurturing spaces for her to self-actualize as she believes will benefit the life she's building *for herself*. There's a way that feminism, unfortunately, re-objectifies the female body in its effort not to. We reduce women to the parts we wish to "protect" even as we critique objectification. It's a very paternalistic, patriarchal, and patronizing gesture. Shay has grown into a full-figured woman. Men and women alike look at her with desire . . . on and off stage. I can no longer pretend not to notice. She has evolved into quite a beautiful young woman. I recall a recent play (Rivera's *Sonnets for an Old Century*)—a role she understated a bit, though she appears prominently in the first scene—her first lines including the repetition of "sex," replete with suggestive and matching gyrations. At Spoken Word events, I witness how she now gives a brief disclaimer if I'm in the room and she's performing a new piece that I may find provocative or sexual in nature . . . but I'm getting used to it. I suppose she's a lot like her dad in some ways. How could I ever exalt my freedom to spit, rap, speak, be and become in the ways I have over the years, before her eyes, and expect less from her? And this is the irony of true equality—one that enables me to take a critical look at all my feminist leanings, and flip them in a way that suggests: "It's her body, and she'll live like she wants to" . . . even if it doesn't jive with anyone's "feminist agenda." About this, I am proud. I experience great pride in the woman I helped raise every time I see her perform or hear about her work from others.

Often, people are unsurprised by our kinship. Shay has not been an object or extension of my own movements through life, but a trailblazer creating a legacy of her own that will surely surpass my body of work, given how early she started. She is a being, full of freedom, with choices to make—some of which I may not agree with. Recently we had a discussion about Beyonce and the mixed messaging lyrically she gives to young girls who "run the world" if through sometimes self-objectifying manipulations. I suggest that self-objectification for gain or favor is, ultimately, "a woman's choice." She suggests "choice," shaped by coercive market demands or by necessity, isn't really choice. It's partially my fault she thinks this way: critically. I'll take partial credit, owning that she very much has a mind of her own—whatever my minimal influence. Most importantly, Shay Matestky knows she has my love and support—something my mother has given to me, despite our differences on certain issues. And isn't this the point of feminism and true equality? That each man and woman have the ability to fulfill his or her own destiny as they see fit, with full control of their bodies, full freedom to fly, sit still, soar? What a life! What a wonderful, amazing, beautifully-ugly, tragic-joyful way to experience it all, accept it all. What else is feminism, if not a commitment to full, human freedom?

book|marks

"Entrusted w/ the cultivation of young minds, if I'm not an inspired educator: barely review assignments, pass things off & students through . . . instead of waking early some mornings after just a few winks to be a man of my word: get assignments back, have a strong lesson plan, etc. . . . . it's time to change professions. Nothing kills the will to learn like an uninspired teacher who doesn't care. I ♥ teaching: Passion." —TTW

A Saving Grace[1]

I encounter them more and more these days as a college admissions evaluator—heartfelt, brave stories by high school seniors who "come out" in their personal statements. The frequency of "coming out" essays or Gay/Straight Alliance mentions in extracurricular profiles are a promising indicator that schools are creating environments in which LGBT youth are nurtured and thrive. Still, these are perhaps the fortunate students. As an educator and youth advocate still very much attuned to challenges to serving LGBT students, I am aware that many environments still choose to relegate the topic to silence or worse seek to "ban" same-sex attraction or social activity. While I celebrate the trends of more tolerance and affirmation in the United States, I don't wish to undermine the critical work that school districts and teachers are still doing to create "safe spaces" for LGBT youth. There is empathetic value in offering an experience-based testimony of my own struggles as a young student in Public Schools and the various saviors who prevented the kind of hopeless, down-spiraling dejection that can lead to LGBT teen suicide. Sharing stories is one way to broach a difficult topic with complex solutions-in-the-making.

I had a very early awareness of my sexuality—a point that is no doubt disputed by adults and some professionals who negate the emergence of "sexuality" for kids under the age of consent. It is double-standard "awareness" when it's common for teachers and staff to make reference to kid-crushes between opposite-sex children, without being able to imagine the viability that some young people experience same-sex attraction as early as elementary or middle school. There is the "heteronormative" assumption that "playing house" is innocent modeling of a healthy sexuality, while any same-sex "play" is resulting not from any difference in orientation but some perversion of normal sexuality. In elementary school, I had crushes on boys and girls—imagined a future where love with either could result in a life together. However, I was quickly and frequently informed that there was only one way to make family; and that my perceived liberty to think otherwise would surely lead me to hell or a miserable existence of silence and torment. It is no wonder that I turned to school as an obsessive attachment to avoid discomfort with a natural option denied me.

---

[1] Published by *The Ladder: Storytelling Across The Curriclum (Fall 2012)*

I grew up a very masculine-identified boy. Little league football quarterbacking and being a kid-boxer were among the ways I avoided some of the bullying and taunting directed at more effeminate males my age. I enjoyed sports. I did not however enjoy the notion that reading books or enjoying arts made me less of a boy. I did not enjoy the peer to peer gay bullying I witnessed and was disturbed even more by the all too frequent cases of teachers and faculty reinforcing the gender and sexuality norms that tormented many of my peers who presented as different. Some of the most insidious, homophobic bullying I witnessed in school came from adults charged with making school a safe space, not other students.

Each time I saw someone thought to be gay or lesbian bullied, I felt an enormous sense of guilt for being able to "pass." This guilt turned into bouts of anger that seemed to come from nowhere, but that were an emotional response to a life where I reprimanded myself for my silence. While I avoided some of the ridicule by being gender normative, the feelings of dejection and confusion were all the more buried. There was no language to discuss how a masculine-identified boy could reconcile feelings of homosexuality, especially in a home where a minister, coach, and former military man was the head of household who defined hypermasculinity as the only way. Images in the media then only depicted gays as frivolous spectacles of ridicule or carriers of AIDS who deserved to die. With so few positive images to identify with, I poured myself into books and became an exemplary student, a good athlete, and the ultimate student leader—thinking perhaps that if I were "perfect," and my being gay was discovered, I would have already overcompensated for the "weakness." I graduated a popular and promising honor student . . . with severe ulcer issues, clinical depression, and a failed suicide attempt. Interviewing at West Point, they asked, I told: not of any sexual relations with men, for I hadn't had any, but I did admit to the mere thoughts about attraction to men. In the military of 1989, so a man thinketh . . . so is he. But I was proud of my integrity. It was the honesty befitting of a soldier. This marked the beginning of a life walking in the light of my truth. I believed as my grandmother taught that the truth will set you free.

Today it is said that "it gets better" for LGBT teens. I am grateful for many saving graces who offered hope and understanding amidst such painful and confusing years. There was an instance when a biology teacher reprimanded a student for making jokes about "nasty people with AIDS." There was an insightful English teacher who asked if I'd read Walt Whitman and James Baldwin—men who I came to understand were gay also famous and writers. I came to believe that I didn't have to die and that there might be something to live for. Twenty-some-odd years later, I've become a beacon of light for others through the books I've published, songs I've written and performed, and speeches and lectures I've given. The climate is a bit more promising today—but not without conversation between educators, not on how to compromise morals or religious beliefs, but how to remain committed to ensuring that ALL children feel safe, loved, and affirmed in our schools. An educator myself, I'm happy to have been that saving grace for students who are sorting through a range of issues, around sexuality and beyond. There's so much our young people can accomplish when they are, first, certain that they are cared for and loved.

An Open Letter to Frank Ocean[2]

Good day, Brotha Frank Ocean

I am a member and founder of the now-defunct Deep Dickollective referenced in the NY Times piece written by James C. McKinley, Jr., and published on my 40th birthday. We achieved a great deal of critical success in the 10 years we moved crowds Bay-area and beyond, and those years offered a platform for continued work as an openly gay-identified solo artist. It was refreshing to be honored for perhaps being a stepping stone in creating a world where you could reveal yourself with a great deal more support than the forced invisibility so many talented gay and bisexual artists have been met with. You present an opportunity to be a game-changer when many have sought a formula for acceptance.

I can't honestly say that I was familiar with your body of work, prior to your coming out letter. Many people assumed that I knew you but I won't front. I should be familiar with you, based on your talent alone, but as an indie artist with little hope that the market will ever honor the "real" of how black men live and breathe beyond the often hyperbolic, braggadocio-filled caricatures we see in media, I'd pretty much tuned out. Still, I can say that I'm proud of you. Your letter alone made me a fan; but on the eve of your highly anticipated release I felt I'd be remiss not to offer my support for the cultural impact your disclosure may have on the youth cultures shaped largely by hip hop and soul music.

I am writing namely to congratulate you for your courage to "let people in" rather than the "coming out" many call it. "Coming out" makes such a spectacle of the simple truth about what love can move one to do. Your letter and your loving are simply the "real" so often referenced in a hip hop that seems to be more committed to swag than seriousness. My good friend Karamo Brown once challenged me to see self-revelation about sexuality, not as "coming out" of hiding, but "letting others in" to your truth. The former is so often associated with shame and secrecy, that I've grown to appreciate the distinction. My reaction to your letter and the responses that it has generated (many affirming) is probably more ambivalent than some might expect. It has become trendy for people to support being real in hip hop about homosexuality, even when little support and resources are put in the service

---

[2] Originally published July 9, 2012

of elevating LGBT artists or supporting a world where they can be heard. Being an ally doesn't mean you don't join the mob who decides to beat the gay down. It's the more active fight, before the fight, that honors human dignity enough to keep the mob from even forming.

Remember that your triumph is personal. You capture the poetry inherent in "the love that dare not speak its name" when you courageously decide to sing it. Understand this: Those who take issue with your sexuality? They have the issue. Please don't confuse other people's "baggage" with your clarity of feeling—beautifully executed in the letter-gone-public originally written in December 2011. Feel no pressure to "represent" anything beyond a brotha who has decided to huMAN up and honor the volition of his heart. Your loving is political because it shouldn't have to be. You describe feelings similar to my 20-year search to find the life-partner I'm convinced I'll grow old with. Remember that as a lover of music, and songwriter, you have the ability, freedom, and platform to represent a range of human emotions and experiences. That said, as much as the market will try to shape who you are into a product, never betray your process. Continue to "keep it real" in ways many who criticize you would have never been able to do. Hold those accountable who say they have your back to put their money where their mouth is: market success requires support I believe you already have and will continue to have. It's great timing. With the President's recent endorsement of Gay Marriage, many are being asked to declare where they stand. Stand for something, brother.

Lastly, when love knocks on your door again, remember: It's not about hip hop, or "realness," or Gay Marriage platforms, or the 2012 election; provided it's even a male who you decide to share your love with. Your song is a truth that, like opening your heart to love, quite simply takes your breath away. At 40 I'm embracing that feeling like I never have before. Beyond beats and rhymes, there is the breath, once broken and labored, that sustains you. Breathe easy knowing you've already arrived and worked hard for the success you'll receive. Nothing can be further from your truth.

Props and Congratulations.

Tim'm T. West

Reflections on Teaching: Notes from a "Papa Bear"

So I admittedly had challenges with leaving "personal business" out of the high school classroom. "Keeping my business to myself" would suggest I have nothing, beyond instructional material, to offer students. And what would English Language Arts or Composition be for students, if I could not provide an example of what one can bring to it . . . even as a question posted, a consideration, a devil's advocate perspective with which I don't agree? I believe in fully engaging material in my classrooms, not as some invulnerable repository for answers, but a living, breathing, and thinking man who processes knowledge through vectors of my racial, class, gender, and sexual orientation identities that shape my worldview. The idea of compartmentalizing my personal life—of sheltering, especially secondary students, from basic details of personal life—has, for me, been pedagogically ineffective at best, an unrealistic double-standard at minimum. I think about the students I've taught over the years and wonder: To what degree has offering a personal testimony or opinion, as an accent to a point of view, ever "hurt" or misguided a student? How many of them have in some way benefited from it? Fairness is something I've always valued. Creating a safe and brave space where disagreements are welcome but where civility and respect are encouraged has created transformative spaces where students of various social, racial, political, religious, and sexual orientations can thrive. I'm my best as an educator when I don't have to worry about being fired because of what students happen to know or "find out," given my status as a public figure. I'm a great teacher with a good track record as evidence.

I thought about this a lot when teaching Composition II as a dual-credit course at a Houston-area high school through a community college system. The course required, not by my own choosing, students to develop persuasive arguments on either side of the "Family Values" debate. I've encouraged many students whose opinions I don't share to strengthen their arguments . . . and offered some strategies for how to do that. Many things I don't agree with are grounded in logic that makes sense. In the balance of my conviction, I can agree to disagree while honoring that a great point was made that gave me pause. Helping students shape arguments against Gay Marriage wasn't always an easy task, but sharpened my own intellectual faculties and allowed me to engage points of view I don't at all agree with. It was a source for relating to differences when I was also able to assert my personal belief about an issue.

Am I "out" in the classroom? I haven't made an announcement (in this case) . . . at least with the high school students, because of fear that it would come back to haunt me. I am, however, stridently honest when I find a perspective to be "weak". . . even ones I agree with. I have been "out" before, not as a first day introduction, but when the topic emerged and I felt that disclosure might offer a perspective that might respectably offer an experiential counterpoint. I recall an instance when teaching at a different high school in Washington, D.C. It was mid-term when a "faggot" shouting match ensued in the class. I didn't yell or scream. I calmly engaged students about why that wasn't appropriate and might be hurtful to peers who might be LGBTQ . . . to which the students responded: "Nobody in the class is a 'faggot,' so it shouldn't matter." After trying some other methods and dancing around, my decision to "come out" (safeguarded, in advance, by my principal at the time and one of the greatest educators I know) was met with about 2 minutes of shock and awe, then back to "what's for homework tomorrow?" minutes after. I was offering examples about other people who might be hurt by the incident. I even tried talking about hypothetical or actual friends who are gay and whom I support, but that wasn't working. I even tried to assert that there may be students in the class who were LGBTQ and hurt by the incident though fearful of saying so, but no. Those words hurt me; the big strong black man who helped coach Varsity Basketball and supported Hip Hop and Spoken Word workshops. I knew ultimately that the most convincing way to get student to think about the impact of their words was to be brave and disclose my sexual orientation.

I *did* notice how especially black males' perception of me shifted after, and not necessarily for the worse. They shifted their language about young women they expressed romantic interests for, and they were more kind and respectful to male peers who didn't carry the typical hyperbolic machismo we see in many of our urban schools. They are better men now for it, and also to the women in their lives, as well as to each other. A most proud moment was later in the second semester when a new student entered the class and called someone a "faggot" and one of the young men I reprimanded nudged him and said: "We don't do that here, yo . . . " I didn't even have to intervene. Advancing an affirming space for all was the new norm among my kids at that institution. Climate change in our schools can sometimes start with a brave example; but if our educators are afraid to be out, or cannot (given laws or policies), how can we expect self-affirming students to embrace all of who they are?

Education in America should be about the development of a critical lens that does not divorce experience from "fact." Counter-histories and revisionist projects seek to "set the record straight," which is impossible, if you ask me. The demand for a "once-and-for-all" truth poses the possibility of shutting down and/or marginalizing the voices that, too, have valid perspectives that lead us all closer to truth. Learning is about being exposed to a vast body of opinions and experiences that students will encounter in their lives after. I carry no shame that I've prepared students well for that. Even when it has meant second guessing my efficacy as an instructor, or feeling emotionally stifled with all the worry about "who finds out what." I walked into fingerprinting offices each year I taught with a smile—proud and expectant of a clean record. I've never harmed a young person. I protect them like my own.

Is there a place where I can teach and fully respectably be myself without fear that someone will take the encouragement of "critical thinking" for some sort of lazy indoctrination (which I'd be the first to criticize)? Truth is . . . I love my Christian students, and Muslim students, and Atheist students. I love the straight and gay ones . . . and the ones who haven't figured it out. I respect their humanity. I'm most challenged by the ones I can't encourage to be excited about learning, and most feel disappointed when I have a day where hands aren't flying up and kids excited about the process. So does it matter that I make rap songs about gender or sexual orientation equality—that I do have some notions of social justice that I work, outside of the classroom, to preserve?

I think that perhaps some naysayers forget that I've been a student; and all teachers have been. As an educator I've experienced colleagues who pronounce their orientations each time they mention wife, husband, boyfriend, kids. And I don't have a problem with that. Students who see their educators as fully human, I have found, are more likely to entrust them as real repositories for knowledge. I've taught hundreds at this point who I think would agree. And yet I've felt professionally stifled by a culture that discourages, at best, the kind of human intervention that rather than "shelter" students from the dangers of the real world by not being "real" with them, exposes them (sometimes without proper guidance) to the crude realities and dangers of life after high school or college. I'm interested in finding a way to explore these and other pedagogical issues in a way that has impress beyond a singular classroom. I think my legacy calls for it, and now am in a position to impact thousands of teachers and their classrooms.

Interestingly, some of my favorite educators were taught by me. I'm very proud of them, and I believe that some shining example of discernment about personal matters is something I've carefully managed in being an example to them. I don't pretend to be wrong or right about everything; perhaps somewhere in between. I'm finding my way as a life-long educator who'd put a hurtin' on anyone who'd try to hurt students I care for in *any* manner. I got the tag "papa bear" for a reason. It's a paternal, nurturing energy, or so I was told by students I've taught. It seeks to guide, with kindness, open minds, hearts, and a world we make better, because we believe we can.

Expectations: A note after a "trying" day in class(es)

Students,

There is sweet futurity in the pregnant pause. Knowledge builds in the silence because this is where the answer emerges in the question. I sometimes ramble in the tradition of Socrates, not without purpose, but because Plato, and Aristotle, and some other necessary being-in-thought also required it. I believe in you. Even as I understand that, for some of you, this is your last semester, a dual-credit obstacle course impeding full enjoyment of your senioritis, and that you'd prefer to wait until Fall and college to "think" again.

While today's class was shorter than most, the period later in the day than usual, I did some lecturing in an attempt to prepare you for a paper that will be held to a more rigorous standard than the first. Many of you listened. Teaching for some 15 years or so has taught me how to measure attentiveness. Thoughtful glares read a great deal different than uncaring shrugs or blank stares. The worst are comments that suggest I have nothing to offer at all. I miss very little. The whispers are especially loud. They stick like Houston humidity until artificial cooling triggers a deliberate disremembrance. They are an enemy to anyone charged to teach . . . who actually cares. Sleeping and heads down are just as disapproving. Unlike the pregnant pause, nothing grows in the space where the head meets the desk except demoralization and disappointment for a teacher who cares enough to try, especially on trying days. I sometimes wish I was not this kind of instructor (could care less). But I have never been careless. I grade myself after each class—a measure of whether or not I give birth, through questioning and sometimes critique, to the the pregnant pause . . . that which generates some-thing: an affirmation that this is why we teach, a lightbulb moment or intellectual awakening, and at best . . . someone who becomes a better person for something small said.

Please consider that just like you need affirmation as students, I seek it too as your instructor. Thanks to those of you who provide it in your thoughtful engagement. I encourage those of you who'd rather be somewhere else . . . to pretend.

This space called learning, your futures, and especially that of your peers who care also, depend on it.

Professor West

Why It's Personal:
mPowerment and Public Health Leadership

Day 1 Journal:

There's sometimes an expectation when you do social services, education, or non-profit youth advocacy that you maintain an (un)safe distance between the services and assistance you provide, and the YOU who is providing the services. Client-centered. Detach. Depersonalize. Don't deauthorize. Catch phrases that are the tightrope the more passionate of us walk daily. I am fortunate to work at a Center where I bring all of me, each day. I am also a seasoned non-profit professional who has learned to discipline my passion in order to preserve its benefits while tempering the excesses. The blessing to do the work can become all too burdensome when you don't leave concern about the young men you work with and their issues at your physical work space. The work my team does isn't easy given the emphasis on scopes and program objectives. Still, there are moments that (re)humanize the work you do, not as just labor OR love, but a balanced labor of love.

During one recent meeting, celebrating recent program successes with the impending program evaluation and site visits, my purpose became clearer to me. Many moons ago, I was a young, black, bisexual, ambitious, creative young man with lots of information about safer sex and self-esteem, but no roadmap. At the intersection of SEARCHING and HOME, I found that I was lost. I began to discover myself when the reality of living was illuminated by the prospect of certain death. Late-June. Gay Pride. Almost 27. Still young. HIV positive now. Expected? Yes. But HIV diagnosis isn't and shouldn't be the expectation; and this is why I get excited about the work I do, the reason stresses never overshadow successes.

Each day I come to work, and most of the days I don't, I get to help guide beautiful, creative, dynamic, and conscientious young men of color into leadership and greater self-efficacy. On Saturday, March 24, 2012, I was proud beyond belief of the diverse young leaders of mPowerment: Prodigies of Pride leading clear, candid, sensitive, intelligent, provocative discussions about their lives, loving, sexing, stereotype-fighting, and winning. Their "5 guys, 5 clips" dialogue utilized brief social media clips from YouTube to forge intimate revelations about their own experiences and that sparked some great conversations about everything from dating and sex in the age of HIV to disgruntlement with our two-party political system. Tired and exhausted, I beamed with pride at their success, with just a few days advance notice to work some magic. So yes, this work is personal! I see aspects and parts of myself in each of the young men I work with. A bit of a papa bear, I sometimes want to "save" them because I didn't have a toolkit to "save" myself at their age: lost and too proud to ask for directions. Sometimes the more you know the more people expect you to know better. But being high-functioning and intelligent are little defense against feelings of rejection and loneliness.

Even I seek help in better serving the young men I work with. I've arrived in San Francisco at the mPowerment Summit and Training to gain some tools I can use in helping direct their respective journeys. At my best, the work doesn't require that I distance myself from the work, but to more passionately understand and affirm my connection to the work. I enjoy being happy. I enjoy being successful. I most enjoy seeing the young men I work with being happy and successful. I am angered when people devalue and stereotype young Black and Latino men who show daily evidence that they are more than "grave" statistics that so often define them. I get excited about seeing the potential of a diverse community of young men of color helping each other find each other at lost and lonely intersections.

The programs and interventions we work through are simply maps to a number of sound paths to health and happiness. At the root of my interest in being a better youth advocate is my desire to be a better human being. I hope to leave San Francisco on Friday—this metropolis where I, some 13 years ago, discovered just how precious my life is—all the more committed to be an example reflecting all the promise of shine a diamond in the rough can hold. mPowered young men know, without fail, that they are loved and valued; these Prodigies of Pride I seek to guide, never lost . . . as long as I and others remain committed to finding them . . . wherever they are.

Day 2 Journal:

Day 2 of the mPowerment Summit surpassed my greatest expectations. For all that I gained from presentations about Program Implementation or Sustainability or the implication and impact of our National AIDS Strategy, it was the passion and sense of purpose of Summit participants that most struck me—a kind of egalitarian connection to the promise of the intervention by everyone from its developers to outreach coordinators. We did a lot of affirming and huggin. It was strangely welcomed given my experiences of detachment with the reasons we convene to talk about prevention in the first place: a belief that death by AIDS is preventable.

In the breaths between program rhetoric is when this becomes most obvious: a level of engagement that I haven't really seen around HIV prevention in quite some time. The young men we serve are colorful, creative, vulnerable, hopeful, and yes . . . sexual beings. There's a rather insidious way that behavioral science makes of young men of color, their breath, pulse, and desire-ability, a thing to be measured—something catastrophically determinable and formulaic—in an effort to manage its mortality: CDC, to be sure, a self-fulfilling prophecy embodied by many dying to stay alive. Ironic that some wonder why the most human some young brothas feel is when they are in throes of passion, touched by something fleshy and visceral, unbridled by devices of protection and fear. What, in the loving between men, can be measured? With no money to save us, how would we save ourselves?

Today, between presentations and lively discussion, I received a few logos developed by young men in the Prodigies of Pride CORE group—designs I believe capture the hope and promise of a burgeoning community who truly believes they are on the verge of something truly groundbreaking. They are not exhausted or disillusioned for all their impatience for magic. They are more interested in joy than prevention. I received a picture of them today that mirrored this potential. For all branding their brilliance could conjure, there will be no greater branding for me than their smiles: brothas who extend arms to hold each other up never let each other down. This image captured the hope between young men who were, weeks ago, not-so-distant strangers.

I believe that mPowement's recipe for success is nothing at all if not capturing the imaginations and dreams of young men who shape it as superheroes defying the nihilism and apathy HIV statistics would suggest. I get to work on behalf of brave souls who remind me that it's okay to believe again, be angered by the injustice of of a system's disregard and neglect, who remind me that it's cool to hope for a dance . . . especially with another, and associate no shame with related desire-ability. Sometimes, consumed by metrics and scopes, I forget. The young men I work with don't let me . . . most often through their shameless lives and loving. Prevention is pretty simple for young men always preparing for their next flirt. They deserve the protection of that joy. I simply offer a few safe options. They get to decide: agency.

I often feel that many in AIDS Service Organizations serving gay men have become long-term survivors, not of AIDS itself, but of an infrastructure that has sought to manage a disease still infused with heteronormative shame. They struggle against a burden of proof that "gays," still disproportionately affected by HIV in the United States, are worth saving. mPowerment is an intervention with a foundation, not in explicit testing and condom distribution, but in the bold notion that young men who love themselves and affirm their manner of loving, will care enough to protect themselves and those they care about. I heard a song and a poem over the past two days that offered some of the more incredible prevention messages I've experienced . . . en joy!

Still, spirit is not a deliverable. Joy cannot be quantified. For all our song and spirit, we are stubbornly hopeful if believing that anything beyond numbers will satisfy this burden of proof that gay men are more than HIV risks or sex that so simplistically defines us. For many rising numbers are simply a indicator of the pathology as hypothesis. Our young men are all too often faces, interchangeable and transitory, able to hold the wait of a time when AIDS is a thing of the past. But until then there is the weight of our frustration. We have to prove, mostly to ourselves, that we are worth saving at all.

When I see pictures of the young men I serve each day, it's one of those moments when the numbers become lite and insignificant in the face of hopefulness I aim to nurture. How amazing it is to have found, not a job, but a movement that is a mirror for this journey I continue to stumble into. God always seems to catch me, pick me up when I forget that dying is an option I relinquished because I wanted, more, to live. I go to work, facing metrics and overly-ambitious targets and all, because I feel so incredibly human trying to be superhuman. Sometimes the young brothas I wake to serve remember to bring parts of my confidence with them by admitting they don't know how and by expecting me to show them. They simply believe I have something to offer . . . and so I approximate the dexterity and bravery they expect. It's hopelessness backfiring into hopefulness.

Back in Chicago, I refuel by smiles. I re-energize when I transform anger into action. I get beyond the what-had-happened-was with the what-we-gonna-do-about-it-is . . . And so we do.

Post e-race ... izm:[3]
a rant about the collective disremembrance of color lines

We're all equal now! Obama's symbolic election in 2008 marked instant proof of racial equality for those riddled with guilt about the unmistakable disparities in almost every negative statistical category from HIV/AIDS or heart disease to breast cancer morbidity rates or home foreclosures. Black suffering is equal to that of white suffering. Well ain't that some equal opportunity?! Many "I'm-not-racist-at-all" whites had been wanting that sigh of relief for a minute, and Obama's election became the evidence they needed. His daughters attend Sidwell Friends, both Michelle and Barack are Ivy League educated, what's there to complain about, black (and brown) people?

I'm especially attuned to this newfound EQUALITY on my DC Metro ride from Ft. Totten in the mornings to Tenleytown where I teach Washington National Cathedral Scholars on the St. Albans campus. The demographics of those getting on at various stops is as statistically balanced as a Gerber commercial. Yeah, right?! In our post-racial America, aspiration is great deal more showy than our shameful reality. We need the black covergirl, the latina-or-could-be-Asian girl, and our standard white beauty in commercials. Equal. We live in a society where ". . . we all just get along," and "some of my best friends are black" is true for some whites, and even white people are fascinated by Tyler Perry movies and can do the cupid shuffle. We have overcome!

I notice this equality no more than when I get off at Tenleytown, with other people of color who arrive with me from more "urban" parts of the city. Many or most aren't faculty or administrators at one of the many upper northwest secondary or post-secondary institutions. A guesstimate is that at least half of the Black and Latino folk who arrive with me there are help staff or cleaners or other positions graciously prepared by the first-rate public school system. It's the uniform. In our equal society, I don't see whites with these uniforms in equal numbers. On the buses going down Wisconsin, they have on a very . . . well . . . "Wisconsin" (and I don't mean Milwaukee, Wiscompton) kinda business attire. But everybody wears a uniform. Even me. I wear my "safe black guy" uniform to Tenleytown. It's the performative necessity of being-and-race in America.

---

[3] Originally published in Edutainer Ethos blog, July 19, 2011

In 2006, I once attended a School Board meeting discussing racial demographics and how better schools were failing poorer children in which one Montgomery County parent lamented the negative effects of diversifying schools—noting that tracking was good, because it prepared our "best" for "good colleges" and that there would always need to be people to do manual labor, cook and clean. This, of course wasn't a "racial" comment, but one about class, though its speaker had little class. Perhaps she didn't notice the crude overlaps between poor and working class people in the DMV and people of color. I didn't say 1966, I said 2006, but i digress. We have arrived. Even if I'm not sure what people of non-color look like? But i again digress . . .

Did I say that I noticed our post-racial equality no more than when I get off the Metro at Tenleytown from Ft. Totten?! I mis-speak. One Sunday I decided to dress down and to do some class preparation at a Starbucks in Dupont Circle. See, they are pushing the gentrifying gays out of Dupont as evidence that "gay is the new black." I thought black was still the old new black! Does that mean the gays are moving to PG county? I'm never gay enough so I can't seem to keep up with these things. But I, again, digress. This post is about race. I'm sufficiently black-acting, I think. Still, the NAACP revoked my black card years ago because I still argue that the etymology of the "N" word suggests ignorance on the part of those who negatively re-appropriated (and mispronounced) it for a stigmatization niggaz bought into. Anyhow . . . so I'm just a colored, African-American, black Negro enjoying my Cafe Mocha whipped with fudgey swirls and working on my rubric when a white sistah engages me in conversation about teaching. I try my best to just keep it simple when I'm in such spaces, generally referring to what i do with broad generalities like "teacher" (to which they "Awwww . . . how cute . . . " which pisses me off), "artist" (which they always assume is theater or dance, never creative writing), or "rapper" (see I would say emcee, but that would just be too difficult, and I enjoy the puzzled looks of how a brotha can be so many things and still manage to be [and these are her words]: "so well-spoken, ambitious, and brave." Well KUDOS!! Some big black man's gotta keep massa's chillrens in order, I do declare. We's equal now!

We're so equal I don't even bother to suggest how it's insulting to say that a Professor of anything is "articulate," "knowledgeable" or "accomplished." My white colleagues are seldom if ever described as such. I've actually asked them. I was dressed down, so it wasn't so much racism, right? It's interesting how white profs and teachers dressing down and working in Starbucks are "having a casual, relaxed workday." I get to be "charming," "refreshing" (why? cuz I ain't robbin' nobody!?), or "talented" (cuz when you're black and smart, you're not intellectual or brilliant . . . any intellectual superiority is reducible to "talent"). Did I mention that I love playing basketball and proudly like chicken and watermelon (though seldom, if ever, together). Yep. Very Black. Almost Equal.

There is one last place that I really really really think shows how America has become post-racial: my classroom. Fifteen or so students of color, a few of whom like to interrogate or undermine my credentials because I started off "too cool" and then had the audacity to demand rigor and maturity. My Duke and Stanford degrees "don't mean nothing," even though some of these students aspire to attend such universities. You see, I'm not all that surprised when white sensibility of post-racialism rears its ironic racist head. I'm most frustrated when students of color you prepare day and night to teach, some of whom don't often see black men in classrooms at all, don't respect the journey and passion you bring to the work. I used to do the suit and tie thing on the first days, just to feign some concern about authority and professionalism, when any fool can dress the part and not know at all what they are doing. I suppose I'm wrong for expecting my professionalism to show up in the experience and knowledge I impart. I think I care too much. Yep . . . those white liberals got to me and canceled out my street cred. Damn.

Yes, all too often, by my own (black students), I am tested: either not cool enough or too cool. Perhaps I'm exhausted with carrying the burden of having to be too many things in this limited space of six weeks to make an impression about how Social Justice and Activism can be facilitated through a broad base of social networking and communication mediums, namely the blogosphere. Things have improved. The students are doing extremely well . . . and 3 of 6 weeks in, we've had more developed and nuanced conversations that have enabled the kind of maturity and focus I'd hoped for. But some days it's still draining. Some days I wonder if one can care too much that we're not quite equal . . . and read the papers and see the stats and see that we're a far cry from a society in which people are judged, principally, by the content of their character. Perhaps the students I'm teaching this summer don't quite get it, being high-achievers. Perhaps they don't know their peers who year after year fill fewer classrooms and more jails for having dropped out, more section 8 housing for having become pregnant, or remain aimless and dejected because they have just given up hope.

Yes . . . many days I want to erase race . . . don't wanna run the race. Want to race to that space people talk about called "post" that is the after-beyond of the reality that sticks to me like DC humidity midsummer. But somehow I find courage to do it. "Brave" she said. Nice white woman. She didn't mean any harm or know any better. Meant well by it. Was telling the truth. I am brave. In equal measure to her courage to converse with a big, swole black dude, on a computer with a rubric, dressed down, in Starbucks . . . whip and fudgey swirls and all.

Why I'm with Teach For America

Geographically, I come from a space between the crude reality of homelessness and dreaming. Among my earliest memories is the move from my birthplace of Cincinnati to Dallas, TX. There was the shifting from project to project until home held little meaning beyond the walk between one site of eviction and the next. Rigging furnaces for winter heat, the kind of shame that carries the stench of poverty on your clothes, and mom's tightening countenance before pulling out food stamps in front of judgmental eyes, marked my early childhood. I knew the world wasn't fair.

In my first year of school in Little Rock, Arkansas, I went to 3 or 4 different kindergartens. I was afraid to make friends, if unafraid to fight. I stuttered. I fought as much as I stuttered: soft heart, hard knuckles. I was great at boxing, but enjoyed reading books more. My dad praised the former and said the latter was for "sissies." Born Timothy, my mother, not college-educated but smart, knew that getting me to buy the sticks-and-stones lie would buy enough time to build resilience for its failure. Don't sweat the mocking: Tim and M, then Tim'm. It was okay. I learned that words did hurt: the "n" word, the "f" word. One I heard in elementary school in the "gifted and talented" classes from white kids, distanced from peers who looked like me. The adjective "smart" said alongside the "n" word, didn't soften its sting. The "f" word I heard at home from a touch and go dad whose hypermasculine militarism and religiosity defined the order of things. Geographically I come from a place at the intersection of survival and unsafe spaces. Home was as volatile as the houses in which we lived.

My community was defined by intense poverty. I made the newspaper as a kid: front page of Arkansas Gazette or Democrat for my dad's fuss about the dilapidated home in which we lived. Thinking back, he probably wouldn't have made the rent anyway. For all their learning-as-they-go parenting, my folks did value their kids getting a good education. My mother always checked our homework and would threaten to call the school or teacher if we reported not having any. These simple gestures, years later, made a difference in my own value for education. A mama's boy, I never wanted to disappoint her. I come from a community of black boys where if you were smart, you'd better hide your report card, or get jumped. White people were smart. Black boys were cool. It wasn't cool to be smart. I mitigated the aftermath of smarts by developing a stout athleticism and cosmopolitan cool. When I graduated salutatorian from High School or got into Ivys or West

Point, it was a bit of a surprise for some of my peers. My friends who had fewer options available to them were especially proud of me. They made me promise to write books and talk about them. I have.

I came out to myself in college, and with uncertainty about what I could do professionally that wouldn't force me to go back in the closet. I was a strong gay Black Student Alliance president, praised for my leadership, but pretty much banned from black frats. It was the first time in my life I'd faced crude rejection from black men and made to feel less than a man for my attraction to men. I avoided the suicidal ideation I experienced as a high school teen by connecting to whoever would accept me as is: some were white, some were women, some were even straight men who dared to challenge the norms by being my friends and allies. I learned there that there are safe spaces in the world. They happen when you are brave enough to share the real ugly stuff, and open yourself to the beautiful people who gravitate to it.

I come to this work with 25 years of activism in LGBTQ communities, and about 15 years of teaching. I taught as an OUT black gay man, without any template for how to navigate naysayers and haters, because I was gifted at teaching. There was nothing I wanted to do more. I also believe that life on the margin of the margins centered my empathy, my compassion, my drive for making life better for those I taught. Of the hundreds of youth and young adults I have taught, they all knew they were loved. That understanding enabled my efficacy and made them eager to never disappoint. I suppose I got that honest. Love is such an amazing motivator for excellence.

I believe that we rob society of some of its best, most courageous and brilliant teachers when we suggest that LGBTQ educators are fine, just as long as they don't talk about it and just do their job. I'm most challenged by this norm because of what we are teaching our kids in the process: that dignity is a privilege for some, and shame, the default especially for those at the intersection of poverty and queer identities. We do our students a disservice if we perpetuate the notion that not having a strong and positive sense of identity has no bearing on the kind of future one can have. I'd like to think that educators cultivate, not just healthy minds, but healthy spirits. I joined this movement because I almost didn't make it. Mouth full and choking on aspirin at 16: a lame overdose that was not as strong as my body's rejection. I didn't really want to die. I wanted to be accepted for something I could not change, after fasts and prayers, self-badgering, and compulsory experiments with heterosexuality.

I joined this movement because I almost didn't teach: feeling that being exposed as a "gay" teacher would land me in jail or vilified. Unfortunately, even in 2014, many who feel called to teach worry about the same thing. I joined this movement because there's someone who will have a positive impact on lots of kids' lives and who deserves an opportunity to make it too. I'm happy that Teach For America sees value in having an Initiative that truly says all our low-income students deserve better. Yes, even the "gay" ones.

Inspiration as Intervention[4]
Cornelius Jones, Jr., interviews Tim'm T. West

CJJ: What prompted you to do the work you do now? Also what prompted you to write *Red Dirt Revival* and *Flirting*?

TTW: The question of the work I do now is somewhat challenging as someone who currently coordinates activities at a drop-in center for Young black gay men, teaches part-time as an Adjunct Professor in Philosophy, and continues to maintain a rather active creative career as an author, poet, and hip hop artist. I suppose the easiest answer to the question of prompting would be to suggest that I've always believed this "work" (and all of it) to be my calling. I want to effect change through as many mediums as possible. With writing as my base, there are times when the "work" manifests as a poem, hip hop music, or a grant proposal. I did lots of schooling to gain the capacity to improve not just the quality of my life, but also the communities to which I am attached. As poetic memoirs, my books *Red Dirt Revival* and *Flirting* are simply extensions of my journey. It is worth noting that *Red Dirt Revival* was largely written in response to discovering that I was living with HIV/AIDS. I simply wanted to leave a brave testimony for all I hadn't previously found the courage to say. Then a few years and albums later, you realize that you're actually still alive and kicking, so you continue the work, though perhaps without the same acute sense of urgency that existed in the first "work." I think that this is what makes my authorial debut special, though I think the writing is better in more recent projects. It wasn't supposed to happen at all and did. It was my version of Bill T. Jones' "Still Here" in a (sub)culture where I'd seen other black OUT gay activists transitioning due to HIV/AIDS.

CJJ: I consider your work, especially your poetry and performance poetry, an "act of intervention" and "transformational." Reading your work and seeing some of your work live has been interventional in my walk with my being young, black, gay, and HIV positive and I feel it has been transformational for my life (you are a Hero of mine Tim'm .

---

[4] In 2010, when this interview was conducted, my friend Cornelius Jones, Jr. was completing his M.A. degree in Dramatic Writing, Educational Theater, and Performance. For the essay/research portion of his thesis he was examining the artistic works of black gay men in contemporary culture. The actual title is: Artistic Intervention and Transformation for Social Change: Examining Black Gay Men in Contemporary Culture through the Arts. I'm really honored to have been an inspiration for such talented men. Cornelius published his first book, *Shadows & Lights: Scenes through Verse and Soliloquies* through my Red Dirt Publishing imprint. Check out his work at: www.corneliusjonesjr.com

. . and that's why I'm still standing today). What is your perspective on your works being an "act of intervention" and potentially transformative for your readers, followers, and young black gay men?

TTW: The interesting thing about my work as *intervention* is that it wasn't the intention. Catharsis first was my personal intervention: releasing it, telling my truth, moving to spaces of revolutionary bravery and love. Once the first book and CD hit, their impacts on people more or less caught me by surprise, for neither my work or music are widely read. I do believe that the nature of the work began to create communities of people who honor the legacy of many of our truth-tellers: Audre Lorde, James Baldwin, June Jordan, Marlon Riggs, Essex Hemphill come to mind. In particular, those at the intersection of ethnic and sexual identities in the '90s were being encouraged to create escapist fantasies for mass audiences on the one hand, or be relagated to independent or academic presses or record labels to maintain the integrity of work that didn't "jive" with the capitalist marketplace. A fictionalized victim story about a poor black HIV positive man on the DL would have had cultural resonance. An autobiographical, poetic, intellectually challenging work about an HIV positive overcomer is not so sexy. And this is precisely what produces the *intervention*, Cornelius. I believe it reads, to those who've encountered my work and performance, as something outside of the bounds of the marketplace, and therefore more visceral and real. In a reality TV culture where truth is so often constructed, my work illuminates those neglected spaces that need to be (re)touched and that touch others. Like you, Cornelius, there are many many other black gay men who've written and performed as a result of my personal work or my work with Deep Dickollective. The intervention is showing people that these stories are worth telling, that people want to read them, and that lives are changed because of them. Imagine writing an AIDS-positive book in a culture where the most popular works of the sort were by authors who have died. That's the kind of gap I hoped to fill. To take the hope provided by life-sustaining medications and OUT black gay men again. We were shamefully running back to closets where our experences were the fictionalized gossip of black tabloids and gospel plays. The intervention is that "I'm here," "this is real', and "I won't shut up about it."

CJJ: Going back to this term "homoaffectionalism," do you feel the term is in alignment with your work? And if so, specifically where does it show up in your poems? And how does it show up in your personal life and interactions with family, friends, and community?

TTW: I have personally never experienced a (romantic) love that endured. To that extent homoaffectionalism has been the primary way i engage my affection orientation. My love for sports and athleticism provides a sanctioned space for black male affection otherwise frowned upon by the black (American) culture at large. My friendships engage an intimacy of longevity in the face of relationships that go as fast as they cum. So those who know me to be a man who writes so passionately about the pursuit of love, also understand that it's the literary fulfillment of an absence. This is nothing sad for me, for I believe that we seriously have to consider configurations of love and affection outside of nuclear models that were not created with us in mind. My work is stridenly masculine at times because that is my gender orientation. I was also particularly interested in creating narratives for young black gay masculine men that didn't feed into the "if you can pass, you will pass" trope that feeds Down Low dysfunction. So when I talk about "hard handed domino slaps across a soft table" or "b-ball sessions in West Oakland," I'm engaging a homoaffectionalism that is more about broad same-gender (not sexual) desire, than gay desire. I suppose I want to encourage, not just homoaffectionalism, but challenge the notion that black men (whatever their orientations) should not be engaging in profoundly moving, passionate relationships with one another for our individual betterment and for the good of our communities. The whole "No Homo" stuff, is another stab in the back of a growing movement of black men, straight and gay, who understand that we need to do something different—that the old black masculine tropes have romanticized thuggery and prison cultures at our own expense.

CJJ: I'm curious to know more about what prompted the poem "faithful" from *Flirting*, which deeply resonated with me. Please share your motivations/purpose/point of view for writing this poem.

TTW: "Faithful" was quite honestly written for my elder brother, Charles Everick, and points to some of those boyhood tropes that, in most contexts, become the rites of passage for heterosexual masculinity, but for me, become the very basis of what I came to love about men (even romantically). I thought about one of my mentors, Cherríe Moraga, who talked about mother-desire as shaping her lesbian desire and desirability. In my writing, I love to play with the line between romantic desire and other male desire(s). I am clear that sex and romance aren't the only ways men desire one another, and that a boy longing for the love of father, a gang member mourning the loss of one of his homies, the spaces like hip hop or sports where expressing forms of affection and desire are, ironically, not stigmatized . . . are all *still* about desire. It sadly reinforces the idea that affection is taboo when we refer to it as homosociality or homoeroticism. It underscores cultural norms that suggest that male on male desire has to be codified for its abjectification and punitive codification. We have to name it so that we can Other it. After all, "real men" wouldn't be mushy or close like that, right?

CJJ: I'm also curious to know what prompted "Unnatural Acts" from *Red Dirt Revival* and "First Flight" from *Flirting*. What were you hoping to achieve or say in each of these poems?

TTW: In "Unnatural Acts" I simply found it ironic that we could be so desensitized to black on black male violence that we can have no reaction to virtual or actual manifestations of black male death (e.g., hip hop shootings/violence, sensationalized "reality" fights caught on video). At the same time some black people nearly have a fit imagining or seeing two black men holding hands or kissing. I wanted to juxtapose acts of death with acts some black people feel should warrant a death sentence. It paints a picture that really calls people out on the insanity of their homophobia and heterosexism, because the logic simply doesn't follow that black men killing each other is better than black men loving each other. Even my nephew gets that. LOL

In "First Flight" I wanted to challenge another of our taboos, which is mental health. We are quick to say that someone "needs Jesus" or is "crazy" while dismissing the real psychological trauma many black men have experienced that needs more clinical attention. Therapy shouldn't be a bad word. Anti-depressant should be a word exercised with caution, but not a bad word. Telling your truth or being in touch with your feelings shouldn't be "gay" or "metrosexual" denotations, but ways *all* men should courageously live. When you have one of your closest friends—a man you saw as big, black, strong, talented, a leader—jump from the Golden Gate bridge to take his life, it does something pretty profound about the silence around depression. I wanted to say: "Yes, I have been on anti-depressants." "I have spent days in the hall of a psych ward for depression." "I sometimes feel like I will break." It is in these revelations that I am hopeful black men will come to heal themselves and their brothas, and therefore, their communities. Broken men can't build anything that will stand for long.

CJJ: You continue to teach, lecture, and perform at universities and conferences around the country as well as perform at various conferences and social events, sharing your journey as an affirming Black/Gay/Feminist/Emcee/Poet/POZ man, how does that make you feel and why do you continue to walk this daring road?

TTW: Quite simply, Cornelius . . . I can't think of anything better to do with my life. Perhaps someday, I'll hubby or wifey up and want more to raise kids and be a house-husband and (second-time around) dad . . . but for right now, this "work" is what keeps me alive, adds purpose to my existence, and I am grateful for the evidence that my work continues to inspire and change lives. What more can a brotha ask for than to have that kind of societal impress? I look at your work, often in awe, and think, "Wow . . . maybe my book or performance had something to do with that." My feeling is that you will experience this too. I remember meeting Marlon Riggs in 1990. I walked around the building at Duke where he was gonna be showing *Tongues Untied* five times to avoid being seen having an interest in the "homosexual lifestyle." Marlon Riggs seemed understated and not fully aware, at the time, of how *critical* this work was to me, at 18, and wondering how to shape my life in freedom, truth, and love. I was pretty damn star struck. He seemed pretty damn tired from all the touring . . . or perhaps more concerned about his health. Still, I think . . . "there just might be a 'Tim'm' out there in an audience with something to get off his or her chest. He or she might be inspired by something I say to create their own inspiration journey." And that's why I find motivation to do it. Our world needs more of it. There is a lot of great art that wouldn't exist if I didn't first find courage to speak. Silence (can) = death.

in|between

"I begin and end my days with prayer . . . and in-between the in-between . . . prayer is simply giving hope its song." —TTW

in between

I write you a poem
each day
between the poems
I write down.
a wordless wonderment
these lullabies I lose
parallel exhales;
are whatever I take in
before breathing
you
in
. . . baritones.

songs wrote
down . . .
are the easy ones.
my mouth run out
of tones
to express
what can't be . . .
wail, falsetto,
run and vibrato
you . . .
so used to them
soundin' easy
you forget
what they sound like
 . . . easy.

the deepest stuff
the stuff
I feel
will stick
emerges
in the in-between:
a memory
I prefer to forget
unable to remember
perfectly.

and the song
escapes
with the moment
so the lyric
is but a longing for
the moment
again
everything else
xerox
echo
mirror
anxiously approximating
this song
this poem
for you
this heaven
we have
so long as it stay
in-between.

perfection
needing no edit
this in-between
you and me
is a moment worth forgetting
for the pain
of its sweet
imperfect
remembrance.
even
the most imaginative
metaphors bore:
for nothing on earth
has ever felt like this
but this.

how does one write to you
when you are the poem?
when the words live on your skin
come alive
when my hands
are too busy touching you
to write . . .

so this is the song
about the poems
I never write.

this song
this poem
a map:
find the place
on your skin
I last touched
trace it
to the spot
where I began to let go
and there you have it

a stanza
a story of me
feelin' you
so intently
words betray
the language
that makes most sense
in the quiet
next to one another
speechless
yet full
of the song
. . . in-between.

closer in the distance

dream with me
and I will wake with you
be sleep to pillow
longing
can make heavy hearts
light
years apart
still . . .
we sleep under the same moon
begin our lullaby at dawn
with "good morning"
perfect possibility
in the waking
hours after
look forward to
the sublimity of dusk,
moonlight, shadow
so cover me
tuck me in.
tonight we are shining armor
the distance
piercing.
we fearless in this
war to protect
our hearts,
kills us
the way we need
each other most
miles away.

we
stir out of sleep
reach back for dreams
we have lost.
wish to enter at kiss
exit at cuddle
where pillows can extend
perfection
bodies at play.

is there any smile
more hopeful
than the one that happens
dreaming?
memories
in the making
are born here
eyes shut to open
to imaginings
we deny ourselves
in the distance.
this touch that stays
for its impress
penetrates
deeper than skin
is the hopefulness
of futurity . . .
becomes us.

so we sometime
wake lonely
bittersweet in this
present absence
this distant closeness
so I feel you most tenderly
sometimes
away.
the closing of eyes
symmetrical teleportation
Oleta Adams | Rahsaan Patterson
both angels that sing
"get here"
and Donnie wails for a *Rocketship*
so we be with
stay beside
hold one another
safely
can feel each other
long as we feel
we can.
materialization in thought
not just any body
matters.

dreaming this way
together
we are wait-less.

celestial bodies
collide   dance   cradle.
soul angels
lullaby a playlist
in the key of love.
in the darkness
love best illuminates
our color.
the scent of incense
channels our lovemaking.
the dynamics of cuddle
the physics of spirit
ensure
we have this
whatever we have
when lonely nights seem
to be
all there is . . .

closer in the distance.

weak moments

I miss you so much
sometimes
my chest burns
my eyes start to flood
the dam breaks
not unlike day
and sometimes
pillows
betray the softness of you
heart beat
misses your ear there
holding its echo.

then sometimes
you call
or think about me
and in the whisper
before your tone
or prayer
push through
to materialize
I am touched so deeply
I grow stronger
than the weak moment . . .
sometimes

yes
sometimes
the closest strong
I feel for you
is anticipatory
breathes in the longing

until . . .

space

I have missed you every moment
since the first moment
I realized
I am gonna miss you—
the moment before you
or me
left
for space.

my body knows
these parts and particles
are what matter
are full of song, color,
and movement.
memory is a faithful pupil
translates a photograph
into feeling
so I well up when pictures
make me remember
what I miss . . .
again.

a sighting
in this kaleidoscopic
wonderment
this spectrum of friendships
and relationality
this undying prism of
touch and go
is how the space
keeps us permanent
how the absence
like summer or snow
melts into skin.
so I won't be shaking you off
anytime soon.
you, now
part of me.

amazing
how this frontier
we call space
remains so very full
so ain't nothin' ever
empty
really
when I miss you most
I look through your pictures
blush back at the thought of you
poke or like some magic you wrote
lick my own lips
hold myself at night
inhale the scent of you
generated in thought.

can you smell it
the materialization and feel
of presence
in space?
can you feel it . . .
the way flesh remembers
an imprint
softens itself
for the next hug?

can you hear it
it is the song of our voices
wailing goodbye
for now . . .
until we miss each other
again
enough to feel the space
fill the space
space the spaces
'til they collide
into the closeness
that is ours.

hibernation
(ref: Nietzsche)

sleeping is magic
defers the burden
of remembering
what the heartbroken must do
to fill space:
industrialize feeling
compartmentalize emotion
for the stoic do not cry
outside
having reason not to.
filling what goes empty
the effortless conceptualization
of a physicist
the burdensome gravity
of a lover's history.

romance being a grave
hand me again, a shovel
the one used to excavate
the promise of forever
the one I will now use
to bury it.
the heart wishes to
disremember,
longs for the urgency
before before
no expediency for
filling hole
again.
narcissistic
warmed by the warmth
of warmth
happy with the simplicity
of cave.

enlightenment provides
little protection
for a heart so exposed

consciousness
being overrated
induces the spiraling
to minimize
anything that felt beautiful
so it don't feel so unbeautiful
lost.
set into motion
won't stop . . . except sleeping . . .
the mechanistic orders of the day
or dreams.

these attempts to shield
in the aftermath
calculating
with all the wrong variables
x upside down
still x, if untilted
is never a plus
is what it is
addition will never multiply.
the pain of mistaking
one for the other?
exponential.

Not wishing to think
nor wishing to become
some existential
being-in-somethingness
wishing to have never known
this thing called love
make me bear
my wait lighter than my hunger
awaiting hibernation
from the memories:
kiss, cuddles, smiles
promises.

fill me
with the joy of
a thoughtless thing
sustained not by what he wants
but what he needs:

a dance
a song
a lullaby
a full moon
naked as earth
one with dust and trees
back to Eden
before any Fall
unburdened

sleep in heavenly peace . . .

morning epiphany in Houston

some mornings
I cannot decipher
the distance
between
longing for
and longing to,
the coffee
not strong enough
my heart
still clinging to last night's wrestle
with pillows
the pieces of my life
displaced
like the sleep in my eyes
edges hardened
needing to be smoothed out
like can only happen
with the moisture
of hug, kiss, and smile.

without fail
the promise of a new day
every day
offers a decode:

"see everything
through the lens of love
and joy will find you."

and so I passed the homeless
roundabout 7am
pondering the blessing
of morning
. . . in my car

dropped off mail
for a job that seems
to never let go
that I hold onto
but have

come home to a modest
but beautiful space
that holds all the promise
of the home I am working to build
and thought . . .

ain't my life good?
tired and tried and tested
but an overcomer
and happy
for not being unhappy
jobless, jailed, jaded
hungry, humbled, or hollow.

and so the distance
shortened
cuz I thought:

ain't I glad I have this life
the one God gave me
happy for the breath of now
ain't I glad I got this life.

latex

there's not enough of it
to keep me from loving you
if love
is protection.
I would bury my skin
fingertips
cuticles
all other pink parts
to feel you
safely.
is my sex drive too low
or my love too high?
which is more the problem?

is it any wonder
I prefer holding and cuddle
to sexing?
privilege your safety
over my shamelessness.
these are decisions
my body
can live with.
feeling you
as nature would have me,
a danger.

if I touch you
all the other ways
will it mean as much?
could consummation
of our passion
be locked fingers
forehead kisses
the cradle I do
to avoid
the discomfort
the reminder
the unnaturalness
of latex?

causality

was blue so got AIDS
which is it, chicken or egg?
Got AIDS so was blue

medicine

how I do it
this not-always-easy . . .
how I keep strong
on weak(er) days?
I think of the joy
beckoning
me to claim
the stuff of dreams
and fantasy,
the weightlessness
my pillows hold
holding them
like a wish.

how I do it?
I keep keepin'
the promise
I make to myself
daily
that I deserve and am
gonna get it
and think . . .

this might be the day
this might be the moment
this might be the year
it all happens.

hope
being my spoonful of sugar
medicine
goes down easier
having something so precious
to live for
something even
one would die for
something
like love.

beautiful . . . aftermath
(for Aubrey)

took everything I knew
then forgot
to remember again,
to make this equation
make sense.
a life of lessons
elementary additions
subtractions
in the years between
high school derivatives
and twenty-something free-spiritedness
to accept
lovers are seldom math prodigies
only experts
in falling.

daily cuddles plus morning kisses
times weekly flowers,
carried the sum
of our most passionate powers
only to realize
that in math
things are still pretty
black and white
my dear,
our loving
no simple equation
we
always
complex.
only a fraction
of our trying
measurable.
free spirits
can't be counted (out)
that way.
ask Einstein.

we loved through problems
without answers
with indivisible
indeterminate courage
crunched numbers
with the gut . . .
long-form
not unlike our tossing and turning
together
without a rule-book.
no algorithm.

so when we sat
to sort things out
the brutal truth
relayed so gently--
your fingers counting my locs--
5 times whatever breaks
to bind . . .
we stopped counting altogether.
hearbeats per minute
don't account
for skipped beats
as our hearts have
so often
since we met.
it is our nature
to love
with unknown variables.

and this, my friend, is us:
continuous
stronger than numerical genius
assured by the reality that
you try + I try = we tried.
and sometimes
you have to remember
a simple lesson
so things don't get too complicated.
this is the logic of our bonding
our magnetic anisotrophy
in friendship growing
on an uneasy axis called hope.

and we are still
loving
and however far we grow
we are still
a numerical conundrum
a mathematical wonder.
no aftermath
could render
a sweeter conclusion.

the rainbow:
the most beautiful
aftermath
of them all.

almost

we were almost.
shows up in your eyes
the way they fear
my shameless look at you
tellin' our secret
out loud.

you
were the could'a been
that choked on your dreams
scared of knight
scarred from the repetition
of hope's collapse
thinkin' angels
are better left
watchin' over you
than being reminded
they have skin
desire the humanizing effect
of touch.

over you
they cannot get over you
for the foreclosure
of getting into you.
you take sadistic pleasure
in a love that lingers.

you
are the one who runs
every time I get close
'cause I get into you
effortlessly
get your soul a-stirrin'
know your gut
is a butterfly catcher.
and you
don't want me
to see you pretty
like you are

inside
soft and wet
like whatever lingers
when we almost kiss.

don't wanna be reminded
you strongest
blushing and spooned
want me to pretend
nothing penetrates you
when I do
all the more
you fighting it.

I
used to be drawn to you
used to sketch you
words painting an outline
of whatever
we might have been
if you'd slipped into joy
and been man enough
to stay there
witness
the best gift
you ever gave yourself
for just asking.

I
used to like the chase,
liked testing my heart's agility
beyond brokenness
a self-made
masochist
braving falls
putting my fragility
back together
rearranging the color
of never
'til it recognized
again.

we
are a mess
dancing around certainties,
like the magic we feel
that we tuck away
for futurity
for maybe somedays
or next lifetimes

though magic, baby
is time-sensitive.
neglected,
becomes regret
the imprint of dust,
photographs
faded,
longing for the remembrance
of I-sight.

we
could have been
something Other.
but you
have always been afraid
and I used to be fearless
but have become you.
so that when you awaken
from the sleep
you believe has protected you
from the perfection of we
knowing I am meant for you
living for the (re)assurance
we will be joined
by the almost . . .
bound
by the see-saw imbalance
of burden and weightlessness
you up
me down
you will, perhaps, understand:
regret
is a role reversal.

I will whisper gently
so you feel the heat and breath
of all the wait I carried:

"tell me
how does it feel
to be in love
to be the happiest you have ever been
to be willing to surrender all
to something
so beautifully . . .
tragically . . .
almost?"

desire|ability

" . . . and some of us are made like this . . . made for this. Whatever deferral pain can exhaust . . . we are made to return to it, seeking a warmth under the covers not made by the stirrings of our own body. And yes, some days I absolutely hate being made this way: my pursuit of it, more often than not, just another lesson. And some days, heart-hurt and all, I accept . . . 'cause God knows . . . God knows me." — TTW

blanket

we are lighter
rememberin'
candy-apple sun days
limb-locked chuckles
and the silences
that lead to blushing
behind a blanket.

we get caught
with smile
on our faces
sticky
and sweet,
wiped away
it still leaves residue
so we don't forget
each other
like this:
men preferring to be boys
escaping man hood
for a moment.

here
we laugh
as big
and unapologetically
as night.
we cover the territory
of cozy couches
broad and shameless
and with cuddle.
there is room
for little else here
bigger than the joy
that remains our magnet.
should we forget?
all we gotta do
is get near each other
to remember . . .

so we chill
like wine
warmed by the energy
between us
we sample for good taste
an array of delicacies
emerging
in the spontaneity
of laughter
betraying
unnecessary subtleties.

we
are perfectly random
like lucky lotto numbers
or gumbo
we
garbage salad with catfish
savoring the flavor
the two make
in the palate
devoured with such urgency
and closeness.

we find time for cover
in the crevices
between now and maybe tomorrow
knowing
tomorrow
may never come;
and so we keep a blanket
over and under each other
tug-of-war
'til neither is too exposed

we
protect each other
being such faithful protectors
if often unprotected
sometimes off-balance
we forget anything
that'll help us remember . . .
our hurting

we
don't have to make sense
to be sensual
can warm ourselves
under a ketchup-colored blanket
fall asleep on the movie
we promise to finish
. . . again
but never do

we
very simply need
an again
another excuse
to picnic, inside
where we are safe
underneath our blanket.
holds our best
during our worst days
tightens the absence
so we feel
present
each moment
we get absent
under this blanket
the warmth between us
lingers . . .
so that we don't let go
and so we don't.

repetition
(or daydreams about my wedding day)

there is joy in repetition
I dream to make it so

"I do" rituals
performed in lonely hopeful places
without audience
without affirmation beyond kiss
is a way we practice
for this pending possibility
refusing to fight
for what we already have
owning this rite
as the right thing to do
loving so shamelessly.

I want everyone there
or no one
because
it makes no difference
and makes all the difference
because I have become a man
no different
than the kid I was
with more courage
to dream,
because mom says
I look great in a tux
have legs
Maasi enough
to jump brooms
have been daring enough
to hold his hand
pray over our meals
in public
because
most of the time
I still fear doing so.

over and again
I dream people who love me
will celebrate
the love that found me
baritone and chocolate
like me
strong and soft
like me
one who will fight to stay
committed
to vows we write
on each other's tongues
with each kiss.
we never kiss the same.

I want a grain of rice thrown
for every instance I believed
"this might be the one"
bring bags of rice
the big kinds you find on farms
that calloused hands carry
throw it at my smile
over and again
until I laugh
say: "ya'll niggas crazy"
am told "you axed for this"

throw it with repetition
'til it cancels out the goosebumps
the sting of tears
in my eye-corners.
let there be
snaps for the kids
MLK church fans
house music and gospel
heat like the kind
that makes us feel at home
the kind that sticks
like daydreams we repeat
having been taught well:
this is what it should feel like
when you safe
and dreams become a home.

courage!!!
(a response to Jill Scott's poem "CAUTION!!!")

when caution becomes courage
when the distance between past pain
and unspeakable joy
blur like 11:59 and 12:01
you will understand midnight
as I do.

this will be
where fear retires for a bit
and a mirror suggests
a love not unlike
whatever beats with passion
in your chest
eyes that gaze
with intensity
at your own
resurrection
of that fearless part of you
daring to begin again
believing
you have never deserved
cautionary indulgence
should never again question
the place for your shoes
at the door
the hanger for your winter coat
the space on the side of the bed
patient for the heat of you.

I have made space
all my life for such moments
have longed to leave something behind
on purpose
to return to.
so if you like with the innocence
of a middle school crush
grow-old-get-married-born-for-this crush
let caution cower

be supplanted by a brave soul
with a heart big enough to know
a stomach need not knot
except to feel this full
a mostly open love
is still, all too closed
and the hurt that changed your life
was meant to be
in order to imagine this
bliss
whatever keeps your stirring
day and night
for God's perfection.

we return to innocence
the naiveté of strangers
believing
we have already loved before
in a different life perhaps
given a chance
to let go
to return
to do this
again
BETTER
without caution
with courage.

tongue-tied

each night
I seek words
not already found
wanting to extend
this journey
called life
so lose them
on purpose
for love is a friend
called time.

there's a language
at the tip of my tongue
that rivers back
forms just before the gulp
so my gut
can push it back up.
some call it courage
others
trying.

he makes it easy
for me to say everything
I need
without words.
smiles
and I'm happier
hurts
and I massage the spot
'til we both better:
symbiosis.
he reads the memoir
of hopefulness
in my eyes.
they dance
sometimes sing
always see
clearly
whatever words
fail in my throat.

patient
for now
one day
holding his hand
or him
there'll be a pause
we'll exchange
more than rings
or kisses:
an inheritance
of prayers, wishes,
crossed fingers,
and pillow promises
make mantra
and ritual
through practice
all the hope
found,
tongues untied
freer to say:
thank you
  thank you
      thank heaven for you.

wait-less

a promise
to love forever
is the ring
I've sized
for years
and never worn.
this ring
is a longing
deferred
echo resounding
for whispers:
"it'll happen
in time . . . "
. . .   . just weight
but this finger
has grown heavy
empty.

regret not being as lite
as whispers, promises
or lies
tell me:
have you ever
been to a jeweler
thought of anOther
as priceless enough
to consider
adding weight
between middle and little
21 grams
of lightness?

considered
spending ends you don't have
to make good on the promise
of a lifetime
'cause your heart was ready
felt somebody
worth it?

ever felt so sure
you told your daughter,
moms and pops
about it?
hoped they'd believe you
when you say. . .
"this time, it's real"
. . . again?

ever contemplated
adding weight
to balance
the waitlessness of dreams
bring life into balance
'cause you believed
this joy would heal
everything before
EVERYTHING. . .
make everything before
make sense
make living seem fair?

have you even
dared to believe
you deserve it?
I have
I will again
I do.

Vow

Allow me to be your paper, blank and without pretense or obligation to anything beyond your truth. There's an endless universe of possibilities to ink here, a bigger tomorrow than I can absorb. Write on this heart, this pulp that has been beat into paper has space enough for all of you. Carry me with you only if you choose. I am always already here. Write our names until the distance and difference between them blur—until we have become as black as our heaven. Let the words fall and cuddle with each other until their intentions dance a rhythm unknown to most but through a beat resilient and familiar in the chests of poets. Remember that everything you could ever write is of God. I will never ask why, because I know your objective is to find a place to hold the sum total of your pain and joy. So I offer, without condition, the top of a page, the cut and edge of infinity, I offer the antithesis of misconstrued words, complaints, or disagreements. Here, where I have become open to one who opens up like me, write yourself truer than others have let you. And when the page is so black that it reflects your smile, becomes your mirror, you'll recognize me, behind you that whole time, waiting to appear before you, lips on your neck forever: our kiss of life.

him'm

he cool like khaki
shoes the color his eyes make
when they catch me blush

lips made for licking
a jazz guitar in waiting
kissing fingertips

unbutton this shirt
unleash the magic skin makes
tasting its freedom

On being-in-love
(a humanifesto for the single)

Being a subject who comes into becoming—through language, thought, the materialization of innate (a priori) and experiential (a posteriori) synthesis—love becomes intelligible in one of two ways. There is a consciousness I have about my experiences in loving as a historical subject. The history made in the present extricates whatever instances enumerate to form a genealogy of Agape, of Eros, of the unnamed and unnamable sensibilities between. We know it because we've known it. And we know it and name it love, not because it cannot be called by other names. These assignments we give to emotionality and feeling are arbitrary, if necessary, signifiers we use to build meaning and inform communicability. We simply have to have something to call it so we hear it at all. So as cliché as words like love come to be, on Hallmark cards, out of mouths, in friendship, or when sexing . . . love is true to the feeling only inasmuch we have assigned it the four letter word. Damn! In those moments, love becomes the best filler to supplant inadequacies of language. Love itself is pre-linguistic. We kill it when we name it. Yes . . . love is dead. We would do better to call it what it is: cuddle, date, sex, disappointment, chance, boredom, in-waiting, nothing better to do than do you.

To not believe in love is to live in denial, for its comprehension is contemporaneous with our agility to conceptualize it. To say we do not know it is to suggest that we've never experienced it. One must surely feel its presence in the absence. It is the double bind of any (supposed) incapacity to understand. IN CAPACITY borrows from its antithesis. Said another way, it is to claim "I don't know what love is" when the statement contradicts the intention. The disclaimer becomes the claim. For the not knowing knows what it is not, and therefore knows. Love is never absent. It cannot be.

And why does any of this matter? It matters because I am writing about it . . . and you are still reading. And somewhere between the words you understand you are hoping to gain insight or figure something out . . . and because even beyond the words you think might be trite, verbose, or all too philosophical, you see yourself . . . reflected in the bodacious accusation that we all need LOVE. From an existential perspective the question becomes "Where is the Love?" (shout out: Donny Hathaway). Surely many a song has attempted to capture its vast dynamism. We sometimes understand it best by defining what it is not: The break up song, the longing song, the songs of death and dying and missing sometimes best elucidate love's location. We are myth makers: give it flesh with a bow and arrow. The irony of a naive baby with a precise aim and arrow says volumes. Pull back. Shoot. Really!? With arms too short to box with God, we stretch to give meaning to myth. And this isn't bad. It just is. Our scapegoating love to divinity or chance is no better. Those "matches made in heaven" that strike and burn, the love at first sight that blinds us to the truth . . . It's all such a mess! And how could love not be when we are? How could love be anything beyond whatever we project in our bold imaginations or calculated constant cravings.

Here's what I think we need to do; especially those of us who have resolved that we are safer not being in love. Disremember love. Make dedicated attempts to forget the unforgettable so that the ways love has failed to stick DO NOT stick. Our fear forms in our remembrance. As surely as Descartes knew cogito ergo sum ("I think therefore I am") he could have infused the statement with "in love" and made as much sense: "I think I am in love, therefore I am in love." And is it ever any different? Has any amount of evidence to the contrary proved false against the stubborn determination of our hearts and passions? We pray for rain, for healing, for love . . . and the intention makes it possible. So love materializes for us in the longing—in the tragic pronouncement that we don't need it or can live without it, we emerge as liars. This is why Teena Marie crooned that "cupid is a real straight shooter." His shooting is justified in the aftermath or the reward. Cupid is our scapegoat for not having to own our intentionality. We are quick to say "he got me" when the truth is "you got you." Human up!

For at a moment's notice, that lil' clumsy baby with an arrow could hover over in an instance when we forget to be conscious and protective. Chance may have it that somebody to our libidinal liking emerges . . . smiling on their good side on a good day. And all that shit we talked before about love being bullshit, fertilizes the rose that is the aroma of disremembrance. It is the fragrance of our most amorous imaginings. We give into it like floating cartoons having become hypnotized by an idealism WE OURSELVES shaped.

To be sure . . . there are the critics and jaded ones. They (re)iterate how horrible love is when they most desire it. I know this because I am one of them. Romantically agnostic . . . which means faith and doubt tango constantly with one another, because neither wants to lead. Iteration offers some direction; provides a modality for control. "No" too many times negates itself. It's the nature of iteration: desensitizes. Becomes boy crying wolf when the bear is a greater threat; yet the nature of the threat matters less than the impending doom. How many bad lovers do we replace with good lovers gone bad? I have a friend who I once loved more than a "friend." He reminded me of my fearlessness—though interestingly defines himself as eternally single so much that he keeps it so. A few days in the year, however, he slips . . . falls just enough to reassert his position. Protection. We seek to outsmart love when love isn't smart to begin with. It's chance. The lucky bastards lucky enough to find the love they seek are just that: lucky. I wish to be one of them. And when love fails, rather than just seeing ourselves as unlucky bastards, we punish our choices. And to be sure . . . we do make choices. But choice does not guarantee accuracy. There are far too many variables to consider. Sometimes it just doesn't work.

Technology provides a futile disengagement in the service of engagement . . . though can be fun when you take it for what it is. Social networking of the romantic or sexual sort further institutionalizes desire in order to avert chance. How do you sort? Does anyone not sort? Make a profile. Describe yourself (as if there is some continuity in what people value knowing . . . and even more so their capacity to be honest . . . especially with themselves). In 2011 we can sit behind a computer and construct identities that are not our own to outsmart and manipulate the love deserved. Some of us sit on the other side of the computer . . . believing ourselves to be transparent and honest when even our honesty is constructed. It's all really a game, right? One does better to go to the grocery store, or church, or a bar. Pray that love will enter . . . and make it so. Assume that if it didn't show up one needs to pray harder or that it isn't the right time. Or maybe we just need to leave it alone. Alone.

I was once one of the self-righteous ones, believing I got it right—applauding and self-congratulating pure luck, attributing it to the calculus of their estimations and analysis. And then it fails. You think you've met the one. You are willing to give ALL for it. But there is no ONE. Love is a shot in the dark that hits . . . so we most often miss, turn the lights on, self-correct and claim whatever we've shot as the intended target. For these types, the end justifies the means . . . until the end comes to an end. Love always comes to an end. This we can be certain of. Enjoy love in its life-cycle. Few are forever.

In summary, I propose that we learn to laugh a little about all this mess. That's why I advocate flirting. "Why so serious?" says the JOKER. Good question before the impending doom. So why not make of this experiment in-loving a capacity for being and becoming more fully self-actualized? Not through rationalizations of its delusions or unhappy attachments to the ways humans have constructed picture perfection. Redirect those energies with the carelessness of one who already knows that if love made sense, we'd find it boring as hell. Let's excite ourselves with its wonderment and lack of discipline. Ever fall in love with someone who didn't know? Is it any less a feeling of love than when they know? Is the feeling in your chest indebted to the assurance of reciprocity in order to feel feeling? Hell naw! You feel . . . so feel. Don't struggle against it. Do not apologize for the stumbles, but also do not blame . . . others or yourself. How productive is blame or shame? Our loving, in existentialist terms, is very much the outcome our self-making. We are fortunate if we find another interested in stumbling alongside us with grace and trust as the glue . . . and God, if we believe in one.

What do I know about love? As much as any expert. As much as anyone who has attempted to compartmentalize and narrow a feeling coexistent with the universe and its energies and frequencies. When you think of it that way . . . when you accept that it sometimes doesn't work out because you don't know what you're doing . . . you can forgive yourself a little . . . slip a little and get back up a lot more. The last time I fell in love I swore I'd been touched by an angel. I would have given anything for it. I always do. And when the angel fell out of love with me, I realized he was just a molester with greedy, lonely, fingers . . . and a ego big enough to think that ambition would make up for whatever was lacking in ability. I have forgiven him, because it is part of the disremembrance I need in order to be a fool enough and try again. If there is a next time—which I am sure there will be—I hope to be bolder. I hope to subvert the tools to understand love that I have been given to other tools, understanding that love is not meant to be understood . . . only experienced. And while I can't see trying today, tomorrow, or the day after, I've got a feeling there's some mythical kid in oversized diapers and an arrow too weighty to carry but with the gift of probability on his side. He'll someday hit . . . on the right day . . . somebody cute . . . on their good side. And at that moment . . . everything I think I know about love won't do me much good at all. At best, I can only hope that I'm smiling back, on my good side, at someone who knows as much and as little as I do: nothing, everything. Love.

revolution, love . . .

revolution, love
is one of the reasons
my ears cling to your words
justice
a shared language
so even when we are silent
I sense the quaking
of your heart or hands
'cause shit ain't right:
Trayvon, Oscar, Rekia, Sakia
color the blues of our rainbow
sometimes
in the mourning
so let's find lullaby.

revolution, love
is the cop car behind
bracing for the stop
exhaling for the let-go
'cause you needn't do anything
to be burdened
with proving innocence
black hands, steering wheel
moving . . .
because I can look at you
and know
you understand
how this unnecessary reminder
stings . . .
so hold me longer
than they held us.

revolution, love
is the archive
of books and manifestos shared
the litany for survival
weaved between
fingertips and ball points
afrofuturism and postmodernism

the ways we need
all these paradigms
even though
they fail the moment we name them
but we name them anyway
needing something
to honor our trying.

but revolution, love
is also when you disremember
the imbalance,
for a moment or a night,
ignore the inequality
put down the manifesto
free your arms for hug
shut up your protest
for a second
so you can kiss me
witness the smile
you always mirror.
we deserve to be and feel beautiful
we are more than our struggle
we are also our love.

yes
revolution, love
is not being a prisoner
to the anger
that can consume you
'til you have nothing left
but what you believe is right.

so let it go
enough to feel human
to feel skin
to dance or smile.

sometimes
your joy, in the midst of struggle
and the fight,
is the most revolutionary thing
there is.

sense-ability
(or the inevitability of falling)

how you know sometime
is God tell you
you can smell it
taste like home
visceral
like soul kitchen to hunger
prayer to need
lullaby or cuddle to insomnia
you know
'cause everything in the world
all right
when they look at you
if just for seconds
and you can't stop
blushin'.

this how you know
for when it happen again?
time stop
rainbows connect you
with heaven
praise dance
on the stage of your heart
you pulse
sunshine a defrost
and whatever Winter left cold
become Spring
brisk like a wake-up rooster
you stir for
breath become your wind
smile surrender
your lips quake
for kiss.

your smile focus
to signify
for when you feel home
it tell you on the inside

the dust bodies make
wrestlin' with each other
the sweat and slick of them
disremember bruise
forget falls at play
'cause forever ain't lost its touch
and this proof somebody still believe
if kinda holding back
if half-contained
like a yawn coming
and you know
'cause you
and somebody else
let go
stretch and arch
taste touch better
smell the fragrance of skin
and wanna do it again.

hope is sense-ability
'cause some truths
can never be denied
even when we run from'em
from ourself
like the judge in the mirror
when naked
and your body show you
what you done become
dare you to love and touch it
and you know
it might be time to fall again
'cause you brave now
feel brand new
chin up and back straight again
love yourself so much
you wanna share you
with somebody else
who show up like sun
after storm
make you forget
you got it wrong before
make you remember
you still got it.

admission

I am
by design
a source for smile
a touch that lingers
a lullaby that echoes.
place your ear
on the lonely spot
of your pillow
if you have ever called me love
and you'll hear me
remembering
I tried.

wrap your arms
around your self
if I have ever held you
and note that the urgency
the tomorrow-may-never-come
is mine alone
can't buy that cuddle
like a bird of paradise
or a card
with somebody else's poetry
can't find my song
as a hallmark.

remember
as surely
as you have ever let me go
that no one else
has ever been a sponge
for whatever pains you
'til it almost killed them
and resuscitated
to try again.

I thank you
for bearing evidence
of my resilience
so accept this admission:

I long to feel lightness
more than I long to be strong
I wish for my heart
peace
for I have fought wars
through heartbreak.
and these bruises I got?
go hard.
warrant the softness
of an angel's kiss.

accept
that while I am much the same
I have changed
love myself a little more
than anyone else
believe in joy a little more
than the gains from pain
and hope to someday
stand
at an altar
another's hand in mine
admit
it was worth this moment too
I was worth this moment:
for two
that it was worth this . . .
assurance
and me,
this forever
that is true.

fall of mankind

he offered an apple
with soft hands,
reached out
painted a smile I swore
would cuddle
and wake with me
wrapped in the sweetest chocolate,
knew my hunger . . .
for my eyes, like my tone,
never lie.

one bite
marked the measure of trust
a pre-vow
poison or sustenance?
and God knows
I would risk my life
to feel full
lips dripping with sweetness
the promise
of a lifetime

but even the wise
get got
for the broken
need healers
are drawn to them.
lips too many times cut
stomach soured
from rot or worm
cloaked in chocolate covered
pretty red skin . . .
I am learning to trust no man
for my own protection

I am learning:
pick fruit wisely
and study the root
sweetness has a source
elemental:

seed, earth, sun, water.
and there is a science
pomology
all things should add up
do not apologize
when they do not.
never relinquish
the proof deserved.

I am learning
coating can be deceptive
every hero or savoir
that has held my heart
has been burdened by
its passionate intensity
has admired it best
at distance
fumbled it when in hands
passed it around
like a hot potato
like an unforgettable
touch and go.

I am learning
a love too strong
is to die for
but will kill most men
so most men kill it
believing
bulletproof souls
resuscitate
breathe again
are made stronger
for the next fall

done with crying
I will not be a martyr
honored for my love
in my dying.
for there is still breath
to fall (again)

no breaking point
for broken healers
those blessed
with courage to try
the imperfect perfecting
of flesh and skin
desiring nothing more
than to be given fruit
savor its naturalness
sometimes win:

tuxedo dressed arms
crossed
an "I do" ritual
both
having courage to taste
again
trusting the bite
taking the fall

evidence II

after we parted ways
there was the evidence
I gave a damn:
the framed photos
your name from my mouth
to my mother's ears.
she may have preferred
a woman's name
but she heard my eyes smile
across the miles.
it sounded like her son happy
so she asks about you.

I've made no mention
of our parting
no different than our dreaming
together
it remained a private matter
and there were pictures taken
coordinated smiles
two shades of chocolate
bittersweet
with the salt of secrecy.
no one will ever see these.
for you
they are discarded evidence
blurred with shame.

my heart numbs
in the after
the hallmark cards you sent
collect dust
the screensavers of you
mock my blind faith
and the other loves I ignored
or deferred
faithful for the promise of you
fall back as surely
as I fell
for you.

you suggest privacy
is not a closet
though both feel like fear to me
and falling discreetly in love
an oxymoron
enigmatic
as these tears of mine
for one unable to claim
he was ever mine.

the lesson
the reminder
is that one
who accumulates no evidence
of you
whose home, heart, and mouth
can say goodbye
without trace
never intended to hold you
in the first place
leaving you empty and empty
the evidence
of your private hurt
reduced
to a public poem.

laws of physics

the weight of this loss
if almost, but not quite
the real thing
is coequal
to the weight of my surrender
if a decoy of the alpha particle
the nucleus around which I created
a universe, a "life"
if an axis
an imaginary line on which I grounded
belief in a good God
and these
are reason enough
to not
"just get over it."
there is no direct proportion
in this aftermath
every day
since he stopped wanting to want
the life I believed *we* once imagined
I have loved him.

have you ever said goodbye
to hundreds of people who loved you
because you loved someone
enough to say goodbye to many
as surely as you were prepared to say
"I do," to one?
burden the car
with the mass of things that matter
books, pictures, music, memories
the uncertainty of forever
a test of good faith
the scent from his last visit
the impressions left
that shortened the distance
between time and space
the echo of
Oleta Adams' "Get Here"
or Sade's "Kiss of Life"?

the dream remains
electromagnetic
love, a centripetal force
affecting good sense
like an eye
over the hurricane
is something meant to be
and not
those who, like me,
choose to weather such storms
pick up the remains
and make do
but we do not flee.

some things
some people
are just made that way
to not
"just get over it"
can a raisin in the sun
become wine?

those who have never
loved like this
who've never felt
the crest of surrender
in the pit of their stomachs
who guard, calculate, caution
the heart's trajectory
more easily walk away
"just get over it"
but none of them have loved
with the surrender
if careless
that I have,
with the intention
of trusting a catch
in the fall

and few of them have gotten back up
bruised, broken, and disoriented
for accelerating
for the cumulative perfecting of faith

so many who worship God
do not trust God
as I have
the Christians tell me
of someone who loved like this
I think I know him better
than they
understand that path
if not moved by pulpits
evangelical pageantry
or gospel about him.

this forget me knot
in my stomach
is far too familiar
with waking for the love of him
moments to the year
to deny the force
of all the beautiful lies
believed
the amplitude of
this heart's oscillation
like a pendulum swing
pushed by the smile of him.

so I will take
all the damn time I need
to achieve balance again
I will own
all the love I still feel
because I don't believe
in lying to myself
to save face
appear hardened and unbothered
if unable to cry anymore.

and someday the force of gravitation
will not be as thick as
the escape velocity
the desire to love again
and be loved well
by somebody, I believe, loves like me
Is the inevitability of hope

so I will try
(again)
as surely as I do now.

this is how I'm made
I am a man of God
these are laws of physics.

fault-lines

the day before we met
was no one's fault
nor was the day
we met
tremblin' on the possibility
of fall or fault
avoiding the dis-equilibrium
that can happen
when a smile catches you
by surprise
and gravity remains the only caution
platonics will nudge each other
lead to nothing
after all
or everything.
so it's not even worth saying
you started it.

collision happens.
you nudged again
as many had
me stubborn and unmoveable
a mountain.
figured,
this time,
"why not?"
smiled back
distance being a safety
you whispered.
I chilled.
it was cool.
nice enough to wait or move for
the joy
persistent
we woke and went to sleep
together
lullaby conversation
an echo:
the greatest love song
I've ever been afraid to write.

looking at you
too long, too softly
told our secret.
your eyes do no better.
though it was, for you,
nothing worth telling
and everything
worth keeping secret.

you being the bridge
between waking and dreaming
I fell into
and accepted my place
shame and hush
or doing too much
my heart is a wailing slave
has a bad habit
of confusing long suferring
with reward.

feel-safe stronger than my fail-safe
prayed
believing again, like a child
God's ears wipe tears
give second chances and ninth lives
after an everything
gets reduced to a nothing.

everything to me
nothing to you
except in a fault-line
called truth
you will take safely to your grave
until your own heart breaks
the earth quakes
and the mountain of evidence
trembles nervously
vomits lava and spits ash
thinking
this collision
could have been avoided
with truth:
you love(d) me too.

is a volcano anything other
than a mountain
too long in denial
of its hot spot and heat
waiting finally
to break
at the fault-line,
a nothing at all
tired of lying
showing
the remains of the break:
everything?

every|thing

"Follow your heart . . . it won't mislead. The heart is where the love of God resides. Many or most fight with the heart, which dishonors and distrusts that love. Everything's always, already alright. Just sit still long enough to see the blessing come to fruition. Worry about it and delay the blessing even more. The heart, a most powerful, passionate instrument, doesn't like being doubted. Let it sing." —TTW

God Loves Me Too!
(a meditation on Christianity)

I went to church today, July 25, 2010. One of my best friends, Freedom Gulley, is pastor of Progressive Open Door Christian Center here in Houston. It's what they call an "affirming" or "radically inclusive" ministry (which always strikes me as bitingly redundant, since ministry should be affirming, but I digress). I do not consider myself a Christian . . . most of the time. I do believe in Jesus Christ and believe he led an exemplary life. I strive more than anything to be Christ-like. On occasion I am led, spiritually, to support Freedom's ministry as his friend, and to be in the fellowship of Others who are LGBTQ in a setting where spiritual safety is advanced. As a non-Christian, there are still "ouch" moments, since I believe that Christ is one of many paths to God and that most of the people in the world (Christianity not being the dominant world religion) are not going to hell because they sought to live a good, kind, loving life but hold Buddhist, Muslim, Jewish, or even agnostic beliefs. In fact, it's perhaps radical to say that I don't even believe in hell. We experience our fair share of it here. My take? Why wait for heaven when we can minimize our hell on earth. I believe God is watching those who wait on the Lord vs. those who work in the spirit of the Lord. It fuels my daily good and optimism to think that my rewards are daily blessings from God. I am blessed especially on days like today: money tight, some anxiety around relationships, and asking real tough questions about how best to carry out God's will.

Today was Spirit Groove Sunday at PODCC—a rather laid-back, fun, conversational dialogue led and facilitated by Pastor Freedom and, this Sunday (July 25th), Lady Winner A. Laws (Dallas, TX). Tracy "T.K.O." Kennedy was a guest artist and provided a powerful introduction in song to the compassionate and ever-present love of God. A preacher's kid, I felt right at home. My earliest memories are of singing "Yes, Jesus loves me" in my dad's church, until convinced as a boy who felt early attraction to both girls and boys, that Jesus did not. The Jesus I loved with all my heart was dooming me to fire and brimstone for a compulsion I didn't ask for and that felt as natural and normal as breathing. There began the spiritual suffocation, the spiritual schizophrenia. I sought to be whole.

In the service, asked if we felt that God loved us, I responded with two statements. The first was after relaying that I tried (unsuccessfully) to end my life as a 16 year old in Taylor, Arkansas. I'd done my good share of fasting, praying, tarrying, and self-rebuke. I came to the conclusion that 1. Suicide is a sin. 2. Homosexuality is a sin. And I somehow deduced that God might offer some favor to me for wanting so badly to "do the right thing" that he would cut me some slack on the suicide. More than twenty years later, it's such crap when I think about it. Not such crap when you consider the teen suicide rates of LGBTQ youth who often have more courage or a better plan than I did at sixteen. In our Ellen and "How you doin'" gay friendlier reality, those rates are increasing.

My first statement was:

1. I realized that faith is when I trust God enough to believe that those who say I am wrong, are wrong.

God knows me, knows my heart, and I am God's perfect creation. If there was any sin, it was to ever think otherwise—to work against God's divine plan to do all the good I have accomplished . . . and then some, as a living testimony. If there is evidence that I have favor with God, it's that I am still here: more than a decade after one doctor told me I had a year to live because of a "full-blown" AIDS status.

My first statement mirrored a second statement, taken from a Haiku that I wrote in early 2010:

> deliverance is
> never again debating
> that God loves me too

I appreciate the way Lady Winner Laws focused on doing more "listening FOR God instead of praying to God." It reminds me of my years of practice with Zen Buddhism and the power of meditation and chanting. The listening also manifests in our everyday activities—the manifestation of the divine in the seemingly insignificant things. This led to healthy debate about how the Bible is privileged as the Word of God, when Jesus said nothing about homosexuality, when there are more than 350 translations of the Good Book, when it is same-sex acts not same-sex love that is most often abjectified, when it is commonly suggested that God has no respect of person . . . though one thing is clear in most churches: People do! To the interrogation of Christians who say "you can't pick and choose which scriptures you adhere to and which ones you don't," Laws stated it best by noting that there are a whole host of Old Testament laws that most Christians no longer follow: "these ordained ministers are picking and choosing as well."

I appreciate Tracy Kennedy's assertion that the Bible is among sources of God's message—imperfectly relayed through people and devices that are, well-meaning, but not always on-point. Both as a kid and adult, logic has always balanced my intuitive and emotional side. Growing up in church, certain things just didn't make sense. Moreover, certain things just didn't feel right. It didn't make sense that we should love our fellowman, just not a fellow, man. It didn't feel right that "faggots and dykes" would burn forever in hell. Wouldn't the faggots (burning wood) and dykes (water retainers) find a way to counter balance God's disciplining and punitive vengeance? Seriously though, my love for God felt good, the fear of God felt scary. Fear became the common tool to motivate righteousness, not love. I can honestly say that I'm happy that my deliverance enables a pursuit of joy, freedom, truth, and love that kick fear's ass every time. Praise Jesus!

Later in the discussion, I mentioned the term Jihad, as someone more interested in connections between different expressions of faith, as one who honors ancestral connections with the earth as what, to some Christians, be considered idolatry, and as a student of God who is humble enough to believe that there is something worth learning about all religions. Jihad is commonly known as a "holy war," but I learned in Spring 2009 at a Humboldt State University screening of "Jihad of Love" directed by Parvez Sharma, that Jihad is more essentially about "struggle." His brilliant film elucidated the courage that many LGBTQ Muslims around the world rely on, *through* their Muslim faith, to sustain belief that their same-gender-loving is God's will. I brought it up with reference to my friend Mechell Brown's Facebook post last week about some people in her life believing that homosexuality *must* be a struggle, if you believe in and love God. The only struggle I've had with my sexuality has been finding and sustaining the right mate.

In 1989, I struggled with the juggle of 15 or 20 or 25 pills . . . coke or water . . . or kool aid . . . in a shivering strong hand. Point guard on the basketball team. Soon-to-be Mr. Taylor High School. Exemplary student, athlete, youth minister, citizen, researcher, and West Point recruit. Though there have been some stumbles in faith over the years, some varied expressions of that faith, I have not, for one day since surviving 2 hours over a toilet and a suicide note I never got to leave, questioned God's love for me. The proof is in the blessings I experience daily, often amidst hardships that some would have me believe occur because God is giving a sign that how I am living is wrong. Well, if punishment is reducible to gay people being unhappy and straights being in paradise, I'm on the wrong planet. I know plenty of gay gays and unhappy straights. I guess we bisexuals are in purgatory, huh? Nonsense! The God I serve is simply bigger than that—blankets us all in the experience of oneness with the universe understanding that everything is God. Every thing. At least that's what I believe. I often feel closest to God when most vulnerable to being, believing, falling in love. I listen . . . And when it has failed, I don't blame God, I recognize that God spoke and I ignored the feeling in the gut. I am learning patience now towards the pursuit of the long-term relationship I desire. I know that everything will be just fine.

It was a good service. I returned home, having rushed there on a near empty tank of gas. I ran out of gas (first time ever in life) on the way back and just two blocks from a Texaco. God is good to me. Lady Winner Laws perhaps summed it up best when she said: "don't confuse disconnect with the church with a disconnect with God. I have never questioned God's love for me." And whether or not I get back to PODCC to stubbornly, if affectionately, remind my friend Pastor Freedom that he is loved and cherished, despite our differing beliefs, there is one thing I will never again doubt: God Loves Me Too!

liturgy

between prayer and praise breaks
he thinks of me
stronger than any rebuke
of blessing between us
I have chosen
not to watch over him
in these spaces
in person
if in thought.

we telepath prayers
safety in his arms
both children of God
and God
surely knows his children
so we were made for this.

my baby has come to need
Sunday worship
like air.
they are for me broken spaces.
I am healed honoring the distance
finding worship
with common people
in common places
celebrating salvation with sinners.

I am closest to God
when with my love
so practice patience.
these altars and pulpits and choirs
are for him
the hurt and healing
the sorrow and song
the thing that
at once
thickens our distance
and makes us close

so I am never sure
I can go . . . there
not look at him
not think of him
be proud of him
out loud
my eyes will surely show
how blessed I feel.

not sure I can
thank God for him
in public
on purpose
before people
who would doom me to hell
having revealed
the open secret of my wonder.

between the prayer and praise break
he texts: 'hey babe"
miles apart
this is our liturgy.
I write a poem
making our ritual
and prayer
public.

others share
in the profound testimony
of God's grace and goodness:

"God has smiled on me . . .
he has set me free . . . "

saints bracelet
(for Barbara Curiel and Felicia Martin)

its wood
polish
and saintly elasticity
stretch to hold a wrist
I once tried to cut
this gift
marks the humble memory
of the stronger.

one Chicana offers it
like a meal
take or leave
but I was hungry
for protection that day
and ate
allowed its teeth
polished, Pope'd, and Madonna'd
to sink into me
to offer whatever blessing
I most needed
in displays of valor
in the thick of wreckage.

another sista notices
my loyalty to this bracelet
on humid days.
me, not a Catholic
associate it with protection
am never naked
for it is with me
love the juxtaposition
it creates against skin
adds color to this hue man
a masculine embellishment
of delicate strength.

faith is intention
giving itself a pep rally
the altar
a pom pom
for believers,
the cheers
rituals or prayers.

so while I am not certain
of what I believe sometimes
I believe in something:
full moons
tomorrow will be better
God is love
if not as specific
as religion requires,
believe that my next smile
might feel better than the last
and is worth
the patience required.

this saints bracelet
full of the glow and grace
of protectors
reminds me.
in the difference between
distance and dissonance
I am there too.

each time I look
for someone watchin over me
there is my reflection
off-center and full of blur
kinda saintly
rememory of
la facultad
given to those
between rocks and hard places.

I am stronger
than I know
for knowing I am weak
just like women
Catholic and not Catholic enough
who see through my toughness
I honor the reminder
worn each day:
twelve saints
I know like I should know Jesus
men and women of flesh and breath
not unlike me.

charming
how we can give faith
to the mustard seed
move mountains
because someone sees us
beyond iconic stature
bravery and resilience
to see we are
a saint
seeking something
in which to believe
a book, lover, a pet, a savior,
a bracelet:
new skin
given to a man
who dares
over and again
to begin.

bruise

hardened
he retains still
a soft spot
a sacred place
refusing
dis-remembrance
of the scar
the point of injury
being torture enough
he wished
water from tears
would be cleansing enough.

this bruise
is where dry tears fall,
is where skin
absorbs the gravity.
if only
heartbreak
carried the logic
of sweat or spit
hard earned
he would
proudly relinquish
this bruise
as evidence
of the body's resilience.

this break
weakens him
the memory stronger
each distancing day
a fine line
between the caress
and applying too much pressure
when the heart has come
to misrecognize
one for the other.

who can he trust
to touch him
with perfect tenderness?
only his own fingertips
measure the distance
between his surrender
and the betrayal
that left him lonely
for feeling.

that spot
soft brown flesh
still vulnerable
once brave
now a bruise in hiding
like with fruit
remains the sweetest part of him
is the palpitating pull
of muscle and skin
wanting to feel whole
again

remember
first crushes
puppy love
the blessing of naiveté
if only
to be strong enough
to try again.

even on Sundays

I am rich with touch
urgent for the sensuality of now
will not deny the way my eyes
make the world naked
today
fleshly, softer
tempting our sweat.

this hunger
is a call from God
desire, a ritual
parallel to prayer
and these lips that whisper
to Jesus
are full of kiss.

these songs of praise
began
with my tongue em bodied
em beded, en joy
so touch me
the deepest, most neglected parts
surrender
making art of sacrifice.

this is my body
broken
taste its wounds
dance to my heart
still beating
place your ear
where it drums
jazz-lick 'til I laugh
like an angel or a star.

fall into me
like tears do
'cause we know God in this
and this is how we know God

perfect
sweet
passionate
and because making love
is gospel
even on Sundays.

Sunday hymn for him

today
God whispers a memory:
the last time I held him
his eardrum and my heartbeat
danced.
the hand in his hair
longed to know its texture
and fullness . . . better.
the other hand
clasped his with urgency.

the hand of God
offers
the perfection of how it feels
to be closer.
held us holding one another:
ménage à trois.

the pitch and air
of his slumber,
a hymn and prayer
I wake with
the days without him
with such perfect peace.
the presence of his absence
is so thick.

today
I thank God for the memory
and for him
and ironic as this presence may be
for all the ways the miles
echo
my heartbeat . . .
faint if resilient
as Biloxi blues
there is reenactment
in remembering . . .
our blessing

heads anointed with oil
the sacrament of kiss and smile
unafraid to cry
for the anticipation
of the inevitable:
we cannot stay . . .
must always soon go.

and is there any greater reminder
that God takes care
any greater example
of grace
than the whisper that reminds
"you are love"
when the miles and days doubt it
when pillows lose the shape of each other
ain't it somethin'?
the agility
to smile about it
this lonely Sunday morning
until we meet
again . . .

Meditations on Jesus Songs

The first sound I remember was probably my mother singing some damn Jesus song. She was the product of a man and woman (my grandparents) who, in their old age, had themselves become a bit disillusioned with Christianity except for "special" visits to church during Easter or funerals. I remember the conversations as a pre-teen with my sixty-some-odd year old maternal grandmother, who had taken a more personal approach to her relationship with God. She spent most Sundays preparing food for our return from church. We talked about a variety of topics, many of them quite secular and non-religious. She was the first person to inquire about my sexual orientation, and had no harsh words, just "be careful, people can be cruel." Some family members have suggested that she was a "good Christian woman" and therefore wouldn't have said that. I agree with the first part of the statement. So my connection to Christianity is nurtured by the memories of a grandmother who knew unconditional love in a way I didn't experience from some others in my family, and stained by the more romantic claims by my family that she wouldn't have accepted my homosexuality. Reasonably, I was quite confused growing up about the damn Jesus songs. I was one of those kids that knew he would grow up to love men as early as I had a concept of what romance and marriage were. Unfortunately, these Jesus songs seemed to signify a painful reminder that my way of thinking was abominable. Every time I heard "Jesus," I didn't hear that he loved me, but that he hated me. It was unfortunate that I thought this way; a preacher's kid with a preacher's wife at home, so the idea of Jesus hating me was a daily experience. Baptism in scripture and gospel music were ritual. So the internalized struggle was in my bloodstream.

My maternal grandfather was often more outspoken about his "issues" with "crooked church folk" than my grandma; so by the time I got really acquainted with my grandparents, and this just before their passing, I was really baffled by my mother's devotion to the Jesus songs. My mom, after all, was the church goer, my grandparents were not. This isn't to suggest that my grandparents weren't Christian or religious, but that my experience of Christianity was shaped by: a black minister, my father, whose actions at that time were harshly juxtaposed to his "teachings," a mother who, without being devout, had a rather subtle, fanatic way of creating scripture collage on every available wall space so that her 7 children would not be "led astray," and my grandparents, aging and cynical, close to death, and as I saw it, less seduced by the ruse of salvation than their children, yet certainly more loving and hopeful about their grandchildren's potential to lead happier, productive lives.

"Moms" still relishes a recording of my muffled 2-year-old breathy baritone pushing out "Jesus loves the little children" before I had any notion of a God who would someday burn me eternally in the pit of fire and brimstone. Listening to that recording, some thirty years after, I thought that even at two, I "believed" in God, believed in the way newborns trust a mother's tit for sustenance. And I grew up this child who loved the Lord. Even as a kid I recall Pentecostal prophecies that I'd be "called" to minister. As I read the Bible, I wanted an even deeper understanding of God's word than my Sunday school teachers offered. As a teenager, I became a bit frustrated with the reiteration of the Bible without application to daily experience. I grew hardened by the juxtaposition of "salvation" and the daily poverty and struggle my family experienced. Yes, the meek shall inherit the earth, but why all the meek people gotta be mostly black and brown? And aren't there other factors besides prayer? Like calling a bigot a bigot? Isn't there something very spiritual about activism and a sense of justice? And if love is so Christian, why would it matter how people made love? This stuff didn't make sense to me, so I kept my mouth shut and prayed a lot on my own. You can imagine why the deacon-prayin', sacrificial Jesus stuff of Southern Baptists didn't sit well with a budding queer activist. My dad's charismatic roots in the Pentecostal Church and his rigid policing of all things secular had this ironic mix of entertainment and rebuke; which wasn't any better: We shouted, danced, sang and felt good, then felt guilty for feeling good. It was a pretty sick cycle.

So I did the logical thing for a wandering postmodern black homosexual in training and became a Mormon. Well . . . it's not quite that simple. When I was about 10 years old my parents were having some serious marriage issues; and it was easier to attribute the problems to their differing denominations than to the excessive abuse and neglect we were experiencing in our family. My dad was less of a pastor then, and more of a charismatic evangelical who couldn't manage to keep a church, but was a gifted orator. Because he wasn't connected to any particular church, he often fell on hard times financially. Dad also had a criminal record from his post-Vietnam, black panther, hustling era, so it was hard for him to find steady work. He was often frustrated and sometimes took it out on us. The Mormon missionaries, for a moment, became the band-aid for these and other serious issues: violence, womanizing, drug abuse, and the related misappropriation of funds.

Their strong sense of "family values" and the nurturing of the Church of Jesus Christ of Latter Day Saints were pretty seductive to my parents. Everyone's seen the LDS commercials: parents and children smiling, families are forever, love love love: spiritual propaganda at its best. My parents actually started getting along and loving each other for a change. So my siblings and I thought, "maybe there's something to this." Plus, the elders seemed to be cool courageous white dudes coming into the hood with their Book of Mormon, so for a period of about a year, we all went to church there (mom and dad included).

The Book of Mormon was like the Bible but remixed for the New World. That made sense to me. But the charm did not last; and my parents started having problems again, so everyone stopped going . . . except for me. Teenage Mormons, for all their faulty-fanaticism and obsession with shame, had lots of fun. As a teen I had access to Boy Scouts, basketball teams, church dances (yes, with hip hop and soul music among the pop favorites of the day). I was like . . . "Haaaayyy! Church!" Black churches had better music and choirs, but I think the intensive indoctrination of my earlier years left me hungry for something different. Mormons were more polite Christians, so I didn't have to worry about being "gay bashed" from the pulpit. It just wasn't their way, at least not where I attended. I would still go to church with my family, but alternated it with fairly regular visits to the Mormon church. Yes, I know: Mormons only started letting black people in their church in the '70s or something, but I got to dance to Run DMC and Madonna at the youth dances. They didn't seem as racist as other white people in the South, in part, because their unorthodox faith made them a religious minority, subject to the ridicule and taunting of "real Southern Christians." I felt that these Latter Day Saints provided an alternative way to stay connected to the God I had grown to love.

Then I came into a greater awareness of what it meant to be a black man in America, and experienced racist parents of white female friends who became all the more anxious as I matured into adulthood. It didn't feel so good anymore because I'd started listening to Public Enemy and X-Clan, so I needed a spirituality that could feed my cultural connectedness. Almost ready to leave the nest and go off to college, I did this zig zag back and forth from the Mormon church to my mother's Baptist church; and all this alongside a growing awareness that my attraction to boys was not a phase. High school years are filled with touchstone moments of dances, first dates, first kisses, and proms. All of these things created great anxiety for me, since I didn't understand why I was not attracted to only girls in the ways my peers were. I hated my attraction to boys because it was clear to me by then that homosexuality was an abomination. When I was younger, I paid it little attention because I wasn't experiencing hormonal changes that lead to greater sexual desire and awareness. The more the hormones kicked in, the more I beat myself up. I was a teenager who, in the minds of many, had everything to be proud of. I'd overcome the barriers of poverty and race to become a good athlete, leader, and student in a small Southern town with few black heroes. I think I probably delved so deeply into studies and extracurricular activities to keep from having to think about how hurtful it was to love a God who planted a feeling in me that he would torture me for. So with no one to turn to, I spent many a night on the "Front Porch" feeling alienated by the very God I'd grown to love and trust so deeply. I asked God for answers, asked if it was really wrong for me to have affection and romantic feeling for other boys. God never told me no. The naturalness of the romantic feeling actually is the closest I've felt to God. But I dismissed what I believed felt right and started listening to my mind. I deduced that God didn't want to hurt my feelings by telling me that the feeling was wrong (he is, after all, an understanding, awesome God). I took matters into my own hands.

I recall fasting for days at a time, hoping that God would release my desire for men. I remember those prayers, hour-long sessions on bended knee crying for God to take the pain away. I had not acted on same-sex desire, but the desire itself was so intense that it felt like I might as well have. At one point I figured that suicide was not as offensive a sin as loving a boy, so I thought I'd try that. The homosexual feeling wasn't going anywhere. I grew exhausted with fighting it; and didn't want to live that way anymore. A few years and an unsuccessful suicide attempt later, my mom started to figure that something was wrong. Interestingly, it was easier to tell the truth about having been sexually abused than to say I was gay. Abuse allowed me to be the victim; homosexuality made me the perverse agent of my own backsliding. This conflicted attachment to church was instantly severed when I decided to "come out" to my Mormon bishop. His comment? "A lot of people have those feelings, you just can't ever act on them." After all I'd been through, I was like "Jeez. Thanks!" But at least I felt like I could tell him. I would have never disclosed my homosexual feelings to the black Baptist minister of my mother's church. Homosexuality, in my mind, seemed to be something white ministers would carefully discourage. I felt the black pastor would send me to a crazy house. And pastors are supposed to be the people we are able to turn to.

I went off to college in the early '90s and became atheist, then agnostic. Blame white liberal teachers and those damn philosophy classes. In truth, I had decided before leaving Taylor, Arkansas, that I wanted to live my life as an open homosexual. When I finally sat still enough to listen to that very same spirit that helped my sing "Yes, Jesus loves me" at two years of age, I was able to develop a different relationship to the Jesus songs. I had sporadic moments when I joined a gospel choir or visited a black church, only to hear more about who God hates than who he loves, so I pretty much stopped giving Jesus a chance. I once started practicing Zen and meditating, but a break-up with my first lover at twenty-one broke my balance and my spirit, and for a moment, I didn't feel that I could believe in anything anymore. Through advanced studies in philosophy, I did come to some resolve about a few things. I believe in something greater than science. The story of my life and my survival alone has no explanation beyond grace of some sort helping me through the muck of self-loathing and rebuke of feelings so central to who I am. At twenty-nine and in Oakland, California, I'd found one church home that was black, progressive, contemporary, and of mixed sexual orientation. Still, while many lesbians were out and coupled, many of the men still felt a need to be secretive about their desire for other men. That this particular congregation could be almost perfect was painfully upsetting, so I even stopped going there. I no longer have hopes of finding a congregation that embodies my understanding of God. . . and I'm okay with that.

These days, the closest I get to God is on the dance floor. My spirit led to dance or weep or celebrate this energy greater than what I can myself muster, some source of strength that exceeds even my own understanding: it is rhythmic, it is redemptive, it is loving, it is the nature and essence of God.

To this day, my very infrequent visits to church invoke the holy ghost. I feel it deep down, I get jitters, a feeling comes over me that is unexplainable, though not unlike those times when dancing when I feel safe enough to weep. And, honestly, it kinda upsets me; namely because I reluctantly and sporadically claim to be Christian. I have sometimes felt that these Jesus song moments are a seductive way black choirs trick congregations into forgetting what didn't feel right about the sermon. As much as I try to shake it, I believe that the God that I was raised to worship hates faggots; and I don't want anything to do with him. I've adopted a polytheistic hodgepodge of deities that love me; it's the meshing of Jesus, Budda, Allah, and Jah with a hip hop remix. It's my very own religion because it provides the safety and unconditional love that I know in my heart, God intends. It's the Yoruba, Voodoo blues that makes me close my eyes when I'm dancing. I retain memories of all the worship-rituals of those who have come before me; beyond my grandparents or even theirs. I honor all of them. I'm quite devout about not being devout. I am the fruit of a people who bowed to symbols and sought witchdoctors for cures, people who believed in working roots on folks and who prayed to a white Jesus to spare their black boys from lynching. I'm all those and then some. And I celebrate this as my own spirited expression of my self-love. The grandmother I remembered loved me because she loved God, not in spite of her love for God. So maybe she and I had the right understanding of God all along; and I shouldn't let others' tainted view of things make me betray what I know and believe to be true: I love God with all my heart and believe that God loves me, just the way I am. After many years of protesting all things Jesus, I'm opening up again to its influence on me. Jesus has become my own personal signifier of my own triumph over racism, homophobia, self-hate, over anyone who would take God's word to represent anything but love.

While I hesitate to associate myself with Christians, I do understand that Christianity is a part of who I am; it's what guides and gives shape to my prayers, hopes, and aspirations. So perhaps I have arrived full-circle to an understanding of why my grandmother, mother, and even me, sing Jesus songs. Perhaps, for them too, Jesus is the signifier for our individual and shared struggles to be good, loving, honorable people in the world. And that's a damn Jesus song my heart, ears, mouth, and spirit will never refuse.

half-full

I who have nothing
will take my next breath
as evidence
that time remains
to acquire everything.

I who sometimes
feel like nobody
will clasp my hands
believing I am heard
by somebody
who knows I am wrong.

I without voice
sing a song of praise
when words
stuck in my throat
require the force of my hope.

I who live with blues
will rainbow my world
a spectrum of crayola
beyond the prism available
through sun and sky.

and yes . . .
I with little faith
will exercise what I think
is my last prayer
in order to enable another.

Kuumba

remember to dance
when you can't find the music.
your feet create sound.

remember to sing
breathless and oft with sorrow
for truth is gospel.

know your art is fine
a portrait of survival
mirroring courage.

your first instrument
plays songs in the key of love
find the harmony.

know that poetry
is what we do with the blues
found in the rainbow.

creativity
is a gift meant for sharing
we heal together
when we lose ourselves
dance, sing, paint pictures in love
find ourselves again.

he|art

"I long ago stopped referring to myself as a hopeless romantic and refer to myself now as a hopeful romantic. Words are powerful. I'd rather be ful(l) than less." —TTW

emergency contact

will you be my 911?
can I rely on you to care enough
to know
should anything go down . . .
you are down for me
whether I'm up or down?
can I count on you for
response-ability?

this simple question
asked at my last doctor visit
made me wonder . . .
who are the ones
who would pick up the phone
at the inconvenient hour
rush to rescue
selflessly if half-awake
heartbeats accelerating
goosebump skin
tears welling
in my bruise, blackout, or fall?

who are the ones
who care enough to know:
T-cell counts
that I breathe with ease
sleep well,
inquire about the regularity
of regimens,
care that I am here tomorrow,
need to hear my voice,
see the way love looks in my eyes
again,
take pride
in my passionate performance,
be #1 fans
and know
I would give no less of myself
at the 11th hour
than the 1st?

partner
best friend
daughter
mother
commitments that go
the way my blood beats
people who know
the tenderness of touch
kiss and hold
destinies purposely intertwined
voluntarily inextricable
each day
trying to know me better
to love me better.
I hope that I have taught them
something about safety
'cause I "got them"
like that . . .

and life is safer this way
knowing
tomorrow not being promised
emergency contacts and others
are the ones
who care to bear witness
to the reciprocity of smile
the dance our laughs do
the harmony of songs . . .
cherish the (com)passion of
the love made
as if there was no tomorrow
today.

will you be my 911?
can I rely on you to care enough
to know
should anything go down . . .
you are down for me?

gumbo

(for those who held me in Jackson, MS)

his palate misses
the 72 hour stew
conjured by warriors
who lay hands on
speak in tongues over
kiss with full lips
share with unsuspecting hearts
their gumbo

a displaced reddirter
longs to lick the spoon
savors being so close to home
that he knows not the difference.
yes, these are his folks
so he laughs a full laugh
slaps his knees
runs out the room.
this kind of happiness
resurrects a child
who disremembers
heart-hurt.

oft mistaken for Yankee
he comin' back
like a prodigal son
remembering his shine
in order to remember his tongue
thick and drawled out
country with little regard
that there's any other way to be

stirs his sugar tea with knives
like it's kool-aid
he recalls spirits that speak
through read clay
in Mississippi or Memphis
studies the imprint
as if it were holy script

dark-palms and full noses
have special sensibility
for their own
prophets

he leaves
almost wishing he never came
returns to the concrete cityscape
from whence he came
questioning
why he ever left home
in the first place
if there was possibility
of feeling so full
in the very place he felt so empty
and alone

he remembers their magic meal
prepared by cornfed, cornbread deacons
singin hyms and prayers as grace.
he relishes the memory
feeling so warm
stirred and watched with careful eyes
like gumbo
licked off colored boy fingertips
who'll miss his boondock bohemian flavor
as sorely as he misses gumbo

A Meditation on Happiness
(for Bobby Dardy)

When does happiness began? Is it that pulse that is always already there, if recognized more fully when we smile or make love? I have come to believe that happiness is a matter of perspective. Cards dealt to us cannot be changed, but there are many ways to play—a series of outcomes determined, in part, by the value of the cards; how willing and capable we are when it comes to maximizing their potential. Given lemons, make Long Island Ice Tea! Many or most just suck on the lemons—complain about the bitterness. Happiness begins when you accept that under any condition, even between rocks and hard places, there is joy in the inalienable volition to choose. Often, love is a lot like lemons: Sucks! Even self-love . . . as clinically "Oprah" as it sounds . . . sucks! You can never get enough of it.

We sometimes pick happiness from the tree of life because it's a reminder that we were not meant to do this "life" thing alone. And we can configure it as romance, friendship, family, or career aspirations but we are social animals who need people. Ever met someone who didn't need anyone? The measure of their joy is evident in their happy detachment. Happiness is showy. It's not the private peace of meditation. Calm and peace of mind are cool and all . . . but they are not happy. Happy makes noise, sings, dances . . . has color and rhythm. But such a needed thing is also volatile; and often the moments that we lose it offer the most critical examples of how precious a thing it is. Einstein, for all his creative and scientific genius, never offered a formula for happiness. And few of us are scientists or geniuses, but surely try . . . it just feels that good. It's worth our time to try to figure it out.

Unfortunately, happiness cannot exist without its opposite. Our comprehension of sadness and loss are in direct proportion to what we experience when happy or joyful. Except there is a third state, ambivalence. Some view it as a safe state, avoiding the extremities of emotionality, but is there a more dull life than not feeling feeling? Doesn't that just feel bad? Yeah . . . I know . . . not as bad as being hurt. Twisted to say this, but hurting feels better to me than numbness, if only because I experience *feeling* alive in it. Feel me?

So sometimes happiness comes in the form of a great love; and for a season, reason (or, if lucky, a lifetime) we are on top of the world. And sometimes it leaves, whether slowly and surely or abruptly and unsuspecting . . . and the loss hurts like hell. And each time you arrive at this intersection of love and loss you promise never to let it happen again. Protect the heart better, be more sure, enter assured of the lifetime. And this is one of the biggest lies those of us who love and hurt hard tell ourselves; whether perpetually single or stubbornly partnered. We mess up because we try not to mess up. Love is not calculus, it's forgetting your timetables or how to simply count. Love is easy. So easy we slip into it like wind into sail or butter on flapjacks. And there are some of us who, bruised and broken, raise our protective shields in an attempt not to submit to the determinism of the divine. We can refuse to play the game and merely spectate for the guarantee of no direct injury. But we still hurt when those we love lose; and we still get hopeful when those we love seem to find it. To be clear, some of us just don't do sidelines or stands too well. We're most fulfilled when *in it*: sweaty, nervous, passionate, driven, ready to win. In the game of love we win if we simply get the lesson. We win nothing by not trying.

There are days when I fall in love. There are days when my heart is broken. There are no days when I don't wish to feel . . . be reminded of the measure of my humanity. Protective, I enjoy being in control of what I have little control over. I know what I can expect of me, if not anOther, so trust is tantamount in any relationship. There are ways to measure trustworthiness. A person does not fail in most life-areas and succeed with you, boo. Do your research about teammates. Look at the stat sheets. Natural talent? Bench warmer? Cheerleader? Most Improved? Most Valuable? There are all kinds of players in this game. I've tried to often to be both the game's hero and referee—letting go without letting go, playing while regulating.

There's a reason we call it *falling* in love. It ain't exactly pretty and is often a bit scary. But falls can be confident. I'm learning to practice the patience to gain that confidence. I'm very good at falling hard and clumsily. And being a bit of an emotional clutz is ironic given that I always feel most comfortable as quarterback or point guard; not so much because I am calling the shots, but because I like the idea of people depending on me. I believe some are born to lead and quite naturally have charismatic and intellectual powers to be sufficiently persuasive. I've been a bit of a control freak: Map out a play, predict the trajectory, SCORE! Captains are uncomfortable when we've mapped the perfect plan and it doesn't work because it goes against our protective perfectionist tendencies. But there is a defense. The defense seizes the vulnerabilities of the offense as testimony of our imperfection. Evidence of God rests with our imperfections. We sometimes get hard lessons so that we are reminded to stop playing God. Loving is necessarily risky and exposes our softest most hopeful parts. There are no guarantees. There is no crystal ball. So why risk it?

We risk love because we can. We risk love because we can't think of anything better to do with a life having so few guarantees. We risk it because tomorrow is not promised. We risk it because even in the thick of our hurt we are reminded of how sweet it felt . . . at some point . . . if fleeting . . . and we are mad it left and want it back. We risk it because there is something in the nature of the human spirit that makes us feel alive in the trying.

We most value breath when it is shortened. We are sometimes not even aware of it until threatened. And what if happiness is like breathing . . . always there, sometimes threatened, because we've taken it for granted. What if the loss of happiness is a reminder that we *can* try all the more vigorously for it rather than give up? When we become attentive to breathing we breathe better . . . We don't breathe better by focusing on our huff and puff—the strained and heavy moments. And what if the same is true for happiness? Focus on happiness folks. Do not get lost in the muck of your pain. Embrace the confidence only patience can bring. Be, believe, breathe, be happy. Meditate on happiness. The focus will seduce its increase.

imprint

the heart
is like mud
in life's forest.
never loses track
of an imprint.

sometimes
we would rather forget
the trial left behind . . .
but how else
would we find our way home
except to remember?

how else
would we find ourselves
except to search
whatever hopes
have gone missing?

realize . . .
as big as the forest gets
as daunting and dark
as nights can be
WE are still there
alive!

memory
is how we know.

golden

silence is the space
between the space and space
is the quiet
before whisper is felt
or before wind
crashes
soft enough
for anyone listenin'
to know
imagination is fed here
dreams play here
uninterrupted
lovers lay exhausted here
so their heartbeats
break the silence
being the body's drum
so shut your mouth!

speak to me
with your eyes
let the symphony of your heart
decrescendo
until you understand
the sublimity of patience.
this silence
God honors with sound
so let's enjoy life's music
quiet with each other
still enough to see
what can happen
when we stop looking
for the words
and let the silence
find us
lullaby us to sleep
understand best
life's noise
for the necessity it is
something to remind us
we are still here.

let us cherish
these moments
priceless yet free
until we are no longer
afraid
of the silence
between us
feel it
'til we fill it
with waves
animations
tune into these
acoustic equations
'til whatever is hollow
sings
echoes
becomes the alchemy
of quiet.

silence
our most beautiful thing
is golden.

skin

my skin
so soft
it might hurt'cha
if you touch it,
or breathe on it
harder than a whisper.

it tender
softer than a baby soft spot.
it always healin'
born bruised
and sen-si-tive . . .
yes Lord . . .
so take care
to take care of it.

my skin soft
and brown-red.
reach beneath
my armor-chest
all that muscle and tough
and you can feel it
pulsin' you to listen
closer than your eyes can hear
louder than your touch
can feel
too bright to taste but sweet
so sweet
it'll stay tied
to your mouth forever
like a forget me knot.

my skin soft
so please, pretty please
be gentle with it
cuz it cut easy
bleed runny
like a cry-baby
or river
so you remember.

touch it
sweetly
and it'll feel as good to you
feelin' it
as it feel bein' touched:
soft
as a fingertip
reachin'
for heat
or magic
sweet and delicate
like skin
especially
my skin. . .

it's a special skin. . .
so soft
it gotta be harder
than anything soft God know
so it survive.

gotta be
the toughest tender
ever
this skin

it stop?
I stop.
so don't stop
this tender touchin'
I need.
bless me
with a touch
as soft as
my own
skin.

lessons in falling: #8

today love appeared
an uninvited bully
so I shot his ass

chicken noodle
(for C.C. Carter)

everything
and nothing.
it was made for this
sits strong
can take the heat
catch everything
put in
so stews
awaiting the dance
between ingredients
bubbling up
on fire
as if to announce:
get ready!

everything
and nothing.
bigger than a cup
big enough to hold secrets
taking the shape
of hands that catch water
it is solid enough to hold
the symphony of salts,
veggies disliked
except this way
noodled in broth
poured to splash
until full
foreshadowing
it is ready!

everything
and nothing.
this instrument that stirs
drums the corner of stove
as if song
as if given permission
to return again

immerses itself
an unlikely alliance of silver
and soup
in stirring and tap
remains a rhythm
this recipe is nothing
without soul
triple-tap to scoop
raise to sip
breath-whisper 'til
almost ready.

And this remedy
is everything
and nothing.
soup   pot   bowl   spoon.
nothing.
without the soul
that orchestrates
goes back to the room
to check on
forehead kisses
and watchful eyes
feet mapping the journey
'til a hand stretches
compelled by care
lips a magnet for magic
this kiss
lips to chicken noodle

everything and nothing
without heart.
would sit there perfectly blended
just-right hot
if not for the soul caring enough
to share in the ritual
proof we are better
we are ready
made
to take care of each other.

apology

forgive me
I fall too hard
too fast
believe my dreams are promises
from God's lips
that cupid
just gotta find
the right arrow.

forgive me
if sometimes uncertain
about my certainty.
loyal to it.
I am learning that truth
is the way freedom
likes to dress herself:
naked
unashamed
glowing.

forgive me
for being demanding.
I have settled . . .
too many a lonely night
in love
breath heavy
praying for lullaby
for the visitation of skin
the resurrection of hope
a honey moon
to cuddle me
to sleep.

forgive this shell
that armors me
when voices grow violent
and loud
or cold with silence.
I am stubborn
believe in fairy tale romance:

we are always
soft
with each other
even when it's hard
like our eyes
flirting with possibility
that we could be
praxis in patience.

forgive
if my loving is
unorthodox
if I wish to share with you
my joy
past or present
of another
who makes me blush.
honor that I wish
to share
the whole of me
forgive if my honesty
hurts
I could not be
but won't.

but never forgive
the way I shadow over you
curl under you
fall into you
be bare with you
worry about and with you
pray for you
hold onto you
to release you
into the freedom two achieve
tried and tested
resolved
in their synchronization
their "why-the-hell-not"
their "nobody-better-to-do" safety
of a peace
neither has ever known.

how to make peace after war

promise
to lay the weapons down
at the door
let only sunshine and possibility
define the landscape of home
hope, the doormat
marked by a collection of shoes
his and his
same size
different styles
know the difference
but sometimes
wear each other's anyway

lay the weapons down
at the door
a sectional and blankets
mark favorite spaces
the textured one
one's lullaby
the smooth one, the other's
remember to stay most quiet here
talking too much
you have learned
a violence
to the language of joy
exchanged through glances
smiles
the unforced touch.
even in this getting-to-know
remember you know each other
well enough
if both still here

don't bring in weapons
from outside the house
when ghosts of the past re-visit
echo "you're not worthy . . .
attractive . . .
ready enough."

don't go through it
warring with yourself
to mitigate the risk
of hurting your other
it's a failed strategy
for it changes you
confidence flattened
eyes full of worry
smile not the crooked truth
either of you recognize
as happy
you won't recognize each other
as love
as sexy
being so unsure.

remember
you can find peace again
if you believe magic exists
if you believe
there are other smiles
like in the best photographs
longing to return
so take the damn weapons out back
even if it means
you begin again
find a burial ground for the fear
dig deep enough
that it don't come back up

and why?
because your eyes
once saw each other as perfect
flaws and all
but started to doubt it
because in the break
there was a prayer
for how full and joyous you once were
not a care in the world
no labels or expectations
just a hopefulness
for the absence of wars
you've already survived.

why

this
is not your fault
or mine.
we tripped into it
running away from,
forgot our feet
prefer to play footsies
over standing alone,
forgot our palms
long for the feel
of fingertips.

so we touched
to regret
having to let go:
a cautious
interdependence.
we know
this tug of war
could end
if we pulled each other
so close
our lips met;
know
we could let go
this rope
we each hang onto
for dear life
and fall together.

know
we'd pick each other up
kiss the bruises
and tug again
needing to hold
this wait
'til it frees us.

you: a tattoo
cannot be lasered away
etched underneath my skin
in blood
I can no longer
distinguish it
from what fuels
the morning's first breath
what propels
the moon to lullaby,
hover behind cloud
'til we sleep.

and no
we cannot be sure
what this is:
fumble to score
miss to catch
fall to fly
and no . . .
it is neither your fault
nor mine. . .

but promise
you'll stay with me
long enough
to figure it all out
long enough
to experience
this miracle:
why.

best hug ever

sometimes
my arms
too short to reach for heaven
cross each other tight
like a girdle
palms sweaty or warm from armpits
both sets of fingers
daring to play piano
at the spine
and I imagine
somebody from God
like an angel
holdin' me better
than I hold myself.

and 'cause I hold myself
so often
so good these days . . .
would that not be
the best hug ever?

About the Author

Tim'm T. West is a poet, scholar, rapper, and youth activist who was born in Cincinnati and raised primarily in rural Arkansas. A contemporary Renaissance man, he is a featured voice in many documentaries about hip hop and masculinity because of his groundbreaking work as a gay-identified hip hop artist, AIDS activist, and youth advocate, among other affiliations. A teacher and cultural producer at a number of secondary and post-secondary institutions, as well as a former varsity basketball coach, West has a B.A. from Duke University and graduate degrees from The New School for Social Research and Stanford University. He is author of several books (*Red Dirt Revival: a poetic memoir in 6 Breaths*, *BARE: notes from a porchdweler, Flirting,* and *pre|dispositions*). West is widely anthologized, and also has produced and released nine hip hop albums, the first several with iconic queer rap group D/DC. In 2013 he released his fifth solo project, *snapshots*. West travels and lectures widely, professionally serving as Managing Director for Teach For America's LGBTQ Initiative, which advances educational equity for LGBTQ kids and youth K-12 as well as their educators.

www.ingramcontent.com/pod-product-compliance
Lightning Source LLC
Chambersburg PA
CBHW031143160426
43193CB00008B/236